Leading Systemic School Improvement Series

...helping change leaders transform entire school systems

This ScarecrowEducation series provides change leaders in school districts with a collection of books written by prominent authors with an interest in creating and sustaining whole-district school improvement. It features young, relatively unpublished authors with brilliant ideas, as well as authors who are cross-disciplinary thinkers.

Whether an author is prominent or relatively unpublished, the key criterion for a book's inclusion in this series is that it must address an aspect of creating and sustaining systemic school improvement. For example, books from members of the business world, developmental psychology, and organizational development are good candidates as long as they focus on creating and sustaining whole-system change in school district settings; books about building-level curriculum reform, instructional methodologies, and team communication, although interesting and helpful, are not appropriate for the series unless they discuss how these ideas can be used to create whole-district improvement.

Since the series is for practitioners, highly theoretical or research-reporting books aren't included. Instead, the series provides an artful blend of theory and practice—in other words, books based on theory and research but written in plain, easy-to-read language. Ideally, theory and research are artfully woven into practical descriptions of how to create and sustain systemic school improvement. The series is subdivided into three categories:

Why Systemic School Improvement Is Needed and Why It's Important. This is the *why*. Possible topics within this category include the history of systemic school improvement; the underlying philosophy of systemic school improvement; how systemic school improvement is different from school-based improvement; and the driving forces of standards, assessments, and accountability and why systemic improvement can respond effectively to these forces.

The Desirable Outcomes of Systemic School Improvement. This is the *what*. Possible topics within this category include comprehensive school reform models scaled up to create whole-district improvement; strategic alignment; creating a high-performance school system; redesigning a school system as a learning organization; unlearning and learning mental models; and creating an organization design flexible and agile enough to respond quickly to unanticipated events in the outside world.

How to Create and Sustain Systemic School Improvement. This is the *how*. Possible topics within this category include methods for redesigning entire school systems; tools for navigating complex change; ideas from the "new sciences" for creating systemic change; leadership methods for creating systemic change; evaluating the process and outcomes of systemic school improvement; and financing systemic school improvement.

The series editor, Dr. Francis M. Duffy, can be reached at 301-854-9800 or fmduffy@earthlink.net.

Leading Systemic School Improvement Series
Edited by Francis M. Duffy

Instructional Leadership for Systemic Change

The Story of San Diego's Reform

Linda Darling-Hammond
Amy M. Hightower
Jennifer L. Husbands
Jeannette R. LaFors
Viki M. Young
Carl Christopher

*Leading Systemic School Improvement
Series, No. 3*

ScarecrowEducation
Lanham, Maryland • Toronto • Oxford
2005

Published in the United States of America
by ScarecrowEducation
An imprint of The Rowman & Littlefield Publishing Group, Inc.
4501 Forbes Boulevard, Suite 200, Lanham, Maryland 20706
www.scarecroweducation.com

PO Box 317
Oxford
OX2 9RU, UK

British Library Cataloguing in Publication Information Available

Library of Congress Cataloging-in-Publication Data

Instructional leadership for systemic change : the story of San Diego's reform / Linda Darling-Hammond ... [et al.].
    p. cm. — (Leading systemic school improvement series ; no. 3)
    Includes bibliographical references and index.
    ISBN 1-57886-167-5 (pbk. : alk. paper)
    1. School improvement programs—California—San Diego—Case studies.
    2. School management and organization—California—San Diego—Case studies.
    3. Effective teaching—California—San Diego—Case studies.   I. Darling -Hammond, Linda, 1951– . II. Series: Leading systemic school improvement ; no. 3.
    LB2822.83.C2L43 2005
    371.2'009794'985—dc22

                            2004015397

Contents

Figures and Tables

FIGURES

TABLES

Acknowledgments

This research was conducted as part of a major study of policy and teaching quality sponsored by the Center for the Study of Teaching and Policy (CTP), with funding from the U.S. Department of Education's Office of Educational Research and Improvement (OERI) under the Educational Research and Development Centers Program, PR/Award Number R308B970003. The contents do not necessarily represent the positions or policies of the OERI or the U.S. Department of Education, or the endorsement of the federal government.

The overarching study of which this was a part was conducted in four states and school districts, with fieldwork in a large number of schools. A shorter version of this research was published by the CTP as *Building Instructional Quality: "Inside-Out" and "Outside-In" Perspectives on San Diego's School Reform* in September 2003. We are grateful to our colleagues who worked on aspects of the instrumentation and data collection for the CTP study that have informed this work, especially Milbrey McLaughlin and Joan Talbert at Stanford University, who were central in much of the design and data-collection work for the California and San Diego portions of the study and who made substantial intellectual contributions to the overall CTP study. Wendy Lin at Stanford University conducted analyses of San Diego survey data on which we drew. Lisa Marie Carlson helped organize the production of the manuscript and facilitated the work in innumerable ways.

The authors would also like to acknowledge the very insightful comments and suggestions of Daniel Humphrey, Richard Elmore, and Patrick Shields on earlier drafts of this piece. Their contributions greatly strengthened this manuscript. Of course, the authors take responsibility for any remaining shortcomings.

CHAPTER 1

Building Instructional Quality: A New Theory of Educational Improvement

During the 1990s, a new policy hypothesis began to gain currency — the idea that the quality of learning could be dramatically improved by focusing on the improvement of teachers' knowledge and skills. As Gary Sykes (1999) described the emergence of reform initiatives focused on professionalizing teaching:

> The premise is that the improvement of American education relies centrally on the development of a highly qualified teacher workforce imbued with the knowledge, skills, and dispositions to encourage exceptional learning in all the nation's students. The related hypothesis is that the key to producing well-qualified teachers is to greatly enhance their professional learning across the continuum of a career in the classroom. (p. xv)

While this notion may seem self-evident, most major reform initiatives during the 20th century have focused on nearly everything but the quality of teachers, emphasizing a parade of new curriculum and testing mandates, more rigorous course requirements, new management schemes, or a wide variety of special programs targeted to students who experience problems in school. History has shown, however, that these kinds of reforms can rarely be successfully implemented without investments in teachers' capacities to carry them off, and recent research confirms that teachers' expertise is one of the most important determinants of students' achievement (Darling-Hammond, 2000b).

In recent years, a number of states and districts have launched intensive policy reforms focused on teachers and teaching, and evidence suggests that some of these efforts have had notable success (e.g., El-more & Burney, 1999; Wilson, Darling-Hammond, & Berry, 2001). But there is still much to be learned about *how* leaders can develop and im-plement strategies to improve in a systematic way principals' and teachers' knowledge and skills, and how these leaders can manage the process of reform in the complex environments that surround school systems today.

This book aims to shed light on this important set of questions through its study of a systemic reform initiative that was launched in San Diego, California, in the late 1990s under the leadership of Super-intendent Alan Bersin and Chancellor for Instruction Anthony Al-varado. In a unique "cosuperintendency" arrangement that has recently been tried with varying success in several cities, Bersin, a lawyer with a passion for social justice causes, handpicked as his partner Alvarado, an innovative educator from New York, and charged him with instruc-tional leadership. As superintendent of New York City's Community School District No. 2, Alvarado had implemented a highly successful systemic instructional reform initiative focused on the professional de-velopment of teachers and principals. Several other districts in New York and elsewhere have since emulated this initiative (see Elmore & Burney, 1999).

Together, Bersin and Alvarado launched a tightly focused, purpose-ful set of initiatives to dramatically improve the quality of teaching in a major urban school system that serves a highly diverse student popu-lation. Toward these ends, they redesigned the district office and local schools, launched extensive and intensive learning opportunities for principals and teachers, overhauled hiring and evaluation of personnel, reallocated funds in dramatic ways, revamped curriculum and instruc-tional guidance, and created a professional accountability system as both a counterbalance to and a means for addressing the state's high-stakes testing policies. And while these efforts succeeded to a consid-erable extent, Bersin and Alvarado also encountered a wide variety of internal and external challenges that typify those that leaders encounter in large, urban school systems as well as in many smaller ones.

San Diego was selected for this study because of its proactive at-tempts to address the quality of teaching, and because of the multi-faceted policies directed at education reform that were simultaneously occurring in California, a state that includes many of the most complex challenges American schools face anywhere. As it sought to reinvest in public schools after years of disinvestment, California put in place a blizzard of policies—some of them mutually reinforcing and others contradictory—ranging from high-stakes testing to new curriculum frameworks, new professional development approaches, and teacher recruitment initiatives. This study documents how one large, urban district developed an aggressive set of policies to improve instruction and meanwhile leveraged, mediated, and sometimes bypassed state policy to further its reform agenda. Within this district and state context, we also illustrate how school-level attempts to reform teaching practice in the classroom resulted in different outcomes in schools that faced distinct challenges under different leaders. As we look at the reform process and outcomes from these different perspectives, we will see that the case holds many lessons for school leaders, policy analysts, and organizational researchers.

BOTTOM-UP, TOP-DOWN, INSIDE-OUT, AND OUTSIDE-IN PERSPECTIVES ON CHANGE

This study followed the reform process at the state, district, and school levels over a 5-year time period from 1998, when San Diego started its reform initiative, until 2003, when the initiative was still underway. Therefore, the story presented here captures the early years of an ongoing reform. During this time, three interlocking teams of researchers focused on state-, district-, and school-level activities interviewed and surveyed teachers, administrators, and policymakers; observed classrooms, schools, central office meetings, and professional development sessions; and collected record data regarding policies and practices.

These teams collectively conducted over 250 interviews and focus groups with teachers, principals, central office administrators, locally relevant community members, and state officials, and observed more than 200 school and district events (e.g., conferences, board meetings, classroom teaching). In-depth school-level data were collected from a sample of four elementary schools, three middle schools, and three high schools strategically selected to represent a range of demographics, leadership arrangements, and experiences; these data were supplemented by interviews with about 20% of the principals from across the district. In addition, our fieldwork is informed by two surveys: a principals' survey (administered to the population of San Diego principals in May 2000) and a teachers' survey (administered to the population of teachers in a stratified, random sample of 11 schools in fall 2001).[1]

Our approach integrates two divergent perspectives that have tended to divide research on the improvement of teaching. One perspective— rooted in the disciplines of economics, political science, organizational sociology, and administrative or leadership theories—entails a view from the "top," or outside, of classrooms and tends to focus on problems of control, accountability, and incentives (Elmore, 1983). The preoccupation of this perspective is generally with the "macro" system in which teaching and learning take place. The second, "bottom-up," or inside, perspective is derived from research on teaching and teacher development, as well as cognitive and sociocultural learning theories. Situated in classrooms, this perspective tends to highlight the nature of teaching and learning, the multiple demands on teachers, and the conditions under which teachers try to engage students in learning (Little, 1993; Ball & Cohen, 1999). This "micro" perspective is more localized, more focused on the individual circumstances of particular teachers and schools, and rooted in considerations of teachers' learning and practice.

The distinctions between these two perspectives highlight a fundamental problem that confronts those seeking to understand policy implementation and impact. Approaches that treat policy as a discrete, traceable set of resources, requirements, and reform intentions emanating from a "higher level" source often tend to lose sight of the way actors at each level of the system interpret and make use of policy events to achieve their own purposes (Darling-Hammond & McLaughlin, 1999; McLaughlin, 1987). Approaches that focus on the fine detail of teachers' or other professionals' practice at the "ground level" often underestimate how larger environmental factors construct and constrain action, thinking, and educational results. By integrating "micro" and "macro" perspectives, we examine both sets of concerns, keeping these perspectives in productive tension as we analyze them within a single state and district context.

Furthermore, traditional "top-down" and "bottom-up" metaphors suggest a hierarchical view of change that, while capturing a common set of tensions, ignores the many environmental forces acting on schools—not all of which are the products of district bureaucracy. The ways in which practitioners experience the world in which they work may also be characterized through an "inside-out"/"outside-in" perspective that considers the classroom and the school as the core of a nested set of influences that can influence teaching and learning. These include but are not limited to policy actors presumed to sit in superordinate status to those in schools. These influences also include considerations of culture and context that have deeper, though often less perceptible, effects on relationships than formal rules or decisions. Thus, as we explore how teaching policy is perceived, used, ignored, and adapted within each embedded organizational setting, we employ a lens that places each setting at the center of an "inside-out"/"outside-in" analysis of policy influences; this lens considers the intersections of contexts and their cultures. Our analysis seeks a nuanced view of how the various parts of interlocking systems may influence one another in environments in which state and district agencies proactively make policy and where schools, too, are agents of practice, reform, and, sometimes, resistance.

While we weave these stories together to look at systemic reform in an interconnected way, we explore several tensions that are raised by one perspective and challenged by another. These tensions tap the age-old concerns associated with collective efforts versus individual needs and centralized versus decentralized approaches (see, e.g., Hightower et al., 2000). They constitute undercurrents in the analysis that follows:

- How strategies address both *systemwide needs,* including equity, quality, and *local differences* among and within schools or districts.
- How agents maintain a commitment to *locally defined goals* in the face of district or state policies aimed at *cross-cutting, externally defined goals*.
- How policies and agents seeking to redefine professionalism as *collective responsibility* for knowledge-based practice rather than *individual autonomy* attend to questions of principled knowledge, local context, and shared authority.

THE POLICY CONTEXT: A BLOOMING, BUZZING CONFUSION

California's Changing Winds

California has the country's largest public-school enrollment, with over six million students in over 1,000 districts and more than 8,000 schools. Its students are ethnically, linguistically, and socioeconomically diverse: Approximately 43% are Latino, 36% White, 12% Asian, 8% African American, and 1% "other." Nearly half (47%) are eligible for free or reduced-price lunch, and 25% are designated English-language learners (CDE, 2001a, 2001c, 2001d). The school system employs just over 300,000 teachers statewide.

Once among the highest-achieving states in the nation, by 2000 California ranked nationally among the bottom three states in average reading and mathematics achievement on the National Assessment of Educational Progress. A RAND Corporation report (Carroll, Reichardt, & Guarino, 2000) noted:

> California's public education system is widely thought to be ineffective. When 40 states and other jurisdictions are ranked according to the reading performance of eighth graders on the 1998 National Assessment of Educational Progress (NAEP), California ranked 35th. The reading performance of California's fourth graders was worse when compared to the rest of the nation. California ranked 40th of 43 states and other jurisdictions on that measure. While the characteristics of California's students differ from those in other states in several important respects, these differences cannot account for California's students' poor performance on these tests. For example, when the states are ranked according to the reading performance of students eligible for free- or reduced-cost school lunch, California ranks at the very bottom of the list both for fourth-graders and for eighth-graders. (p. 1)

An analysis by the Public Policy Institute (PPI) confirmed this view, noting that while California schools lost ground relative to other states across the country in terms of revenues and expenditures during the 1980s and 1990s, California students lost ground in terms of achievement (Sonstelie, Brunner, & Ardon, 2000). After adjusting for the demographic characteristics of the student population, PPI found that California students still perform considerably worse than those in other states on the NAEP, the tests used in the National Education Longitu-dinal Study (NELS), and the Scholastic Achievement Test (SAT) (also adjusted for participation rates). On national tests, after adjusting for language backgrounds, ethnicity, and parental education, the re-searchers discovered that the performance of low-income students was "especially hard hit by the decline in school quality in California" (p. 136).

Following the passage of Proposition 13 in 1979, California's ex-penditures on public education declined markedly. Between 1979 and 1994–1995, the state's spending per pupil fell about 25% relative to the average for the other states, rebounding somewhat between 1995 and 1998 (Sonstelie, Brunner, & Ardon, 2000, p. 90). Although California has a higher cost of living than the national average, it spends well be-low the national average on education both in absolute dollars and as a share of personal income. By 1999–2000, California ranked first in the nation in the number of pupils it served but 38th in expenditures per student, 48th in K–12 expenditures as a share of personal income, and 50th in the ratio of students per teacher, despite the influence of class-size reductions during the late 1990s (EdSource, 2001, p. 1). By the late 1990s, California ranked in the bottom decile among states on class sizes, staff-to-pupil ratios, libraries, and most other school resources. Moreover, the state employed more underqualified teachers than any other state in the country. In 2000–2001, 14% of California's teachers did not hold a full credential (CDE, 2001b), in part as a result of re-duced supply associated with declining salaries and working conditions since the 1980s, and in part as a result of increased demand for teach-ers during the implementation of K–3 class-size reduction in the late 1990s (Reichardt, 2000; Shields et al., 2001).

Alongside the class-size reduction initiative, California launched the Reading Initiative in 1996 in reaction to the state's poor perform-ance on the NAEP. Based on concern among State Board of Education members that the whole-language approach dominant at that time did not adequately teach decoding skills, new standards for student learn-ing published in 1998 emphasized explicit decoding skills based on phonics and phonemic awareness. These skills were to be taught within a literature, language, and comprehension program and sup-ported by ongoing diagnosis and early intervention for students at risk of reading failure (CDE, 2001f). The state standards were accompanied by state-adopted textbooks aligned with the approach embedded in the standards (e.g., Open Court and Houghton Mifflin in reading); state-sponsored professional-development institutes that eventually encompassed the California Reading and Literature Project as well as new reading institutes; and funds available to districts to contract with professional-development providers approved by the state for their approach to literacy. Other professional-development initiatives were also linked to state standards and took a similar approach: for example, large-scale summer institutes conveying a single curriculum to all teachers in a content area (e.g., Algebra Institutes) were organized. These initiatives were implemented alongside policies extinguishing bilingual education (Proposition 227) and tying greater incentives to state tests (see below).

Since 1999, the California legislature also undertook a multipronged strategy to improve teacher quality throughout the state. In addition to small allocations of funds to underwrite teacher preparation for teachers who pledged to teach in high-need schools, increased efforts to establish reciprocity with other states, and a modest boost in salaries, the state invested substantial funding in a beginning-teacher induction program. In 1998, the Beginning Teacher Support and Assessment (BTSA) Program—a longstanding pilot program featuring reflection, formative assessment, and experienced teachers serving as "support providers" (i.e., mentors)—was scaled up to serve all newly credentialed teachers in their first and second years of teaching. In 2000–2001, BTSA served almost 23,000 teachers at a price tag of $87.4 million (Shields et al., 2001).[2] However, many observers suggested that the state's efforts to improve teaching skills were inadequate in scale and internally incoherent, with incentives for entering teaching without preparation outweighing those that would assist teachers in becoming well prepared (California Professional Development Task Force, 2001; Darling-Hammond, 2000a; Little Hoover Commission, 2001; Shields et al., 2001).

These analysts pointed out the many mixed incentives around teacher quality in the state policy system: For example, in 2000–2001, the state spent twice as much money on supports for those who entered teaching without credentials (about $50 million) as on loans or scholarships to support preparation (about $25 million). In addition, individuals who could not pass specific tests could not enter teacher-preparation programs or engage in student teaching but they could become full-time teachers on emergency permits or waivers. The capacities and curricula of teacher-education programs pressured to admit practicing, uncredentialed teachers were undermined by the inability of candidates to engage in student teaching, complete homework, or engage in an intensive, coherent learning-to-teach experience (Shields et al., 2001). Meanwhile, new incentives for teaching in high-need schools coexisted with large disincentives for teaching in these same schools, including lower salaries, poorer working conditions, and less access to mentoring than teachers could receive in more advantaged schools.

While funding for schools and access to well-qualified teachers were uneven across the state, testing tied to rewards and sanctions played a large role in the state's drive for standards-based reform. State policymakers expected high-stakes accountability measures attached to student testing from grades 2 through 11 to focus teachers' efforts on the state content standards and the progress goals defined by the state. Specific policies have included extensive testing (with norm-referenced and standards-based tests every year from grades 2 through 11), a high school exit exam in English/language arts and math (a diploma requirement), and end-of-course exams at the high school level.

Each school in the state is ranked on relative performance statewide, as well as in comparison with "similar" schools, and the state defines a 2-year growth target for every school. Until 2003, the state's Academic Performance Index (API) that comprised these rankings was based primarily on scores on the Stanford Achievement Test, 9th Edition (SAT-9), a national norm-referenced test that was not aligned to the state standards. (The SAT-9 was replaced by the nationally normed CAT-6 in 2002–2003 and supplemented with the STAR test battery, a state standards-based test). Schools successfully meeting their API targets shared $677 million in school and teacher bonuses in 2000; schools that failed to meet their goals were asked to "volunteer" for the Immediate Intervention/Underperforming Schools Program (II/USP). In II/USP, an external evaluator from a state-approved list helps schools take stock and propose a plan for improvement, which the state funds at up to $200 per student for 2 years. Schools that continue to fail to meet their performance targets court state takeover. Policymakers explicitly hoped that the tests and incentives would drive instruction. A policy insider explained:

> So the idea is the API will reflect all these new tests, and then we'll stage-manage it with incentives and sanctions—including the II/USP and everything else. And once we get this grand system into the API, the API will have some real test alignment to the state's content standards and therefore we'll be able to use measurement-driven instruction through the API.

These efforts, in combination with many categorical funding programs now tied to the standards, assessments, and accountability system, have substantially centralized decision-making in a state that had previously been more oriented to local control. As a California Department of Education official remarked:

> We had much more local authority at another time in this state. There's no question that the state, as a state, is taking a much greater role in terms of state direction. Funds are tied to specific programs that come either from the Governor or the Legislature. And I know that's a struggle for many local [school districts].

Following a period of peripatetic policymaking, the budget crisis that hit California in 2003 led to elimination or sharp reduction of funding for many of the programs noted above, including many of the incentives for entering teaching, much of the professional development that had been launched, and the rewards attached to test score gains. This turn of events left a program of mostly unfunded mandates tied to punitive sanctions as the skeleton of California's education reforms.

San Diego's Focus on Transforming Teaching

In this intense state policy context, San Diego City Schools (SDCS) launched what might be considered one of the most ambitious instructional reforms in the state, and perhaps the nation. As the second-largest district in the state and the closest major city to the Mexican border, SDCS exceeds the diversity of this very diverse state, with a large population of immigrant students and higher percentages of African American students and low-income students than the state as a whole. Of 142,300 students in 2000–2001, approximately one-third were Latino, one-quarter were Caucasian, nearly one-fifth were African American, and the remainder were Asian or "other." About 60% qualified for free or reduced-price lunch, while 30% were designated as limited-English proficient.

In summer 1998, San Diego City Schools launched a major reform initiative across its system of schools that continues as of this writing. Two individuals—both of whom were new to the district—led this initiative in what became a virtual joint superintendency. The incoming superintendent of public education, Alan Bersin, had been the U.S. attorney for the southern district of California and southwest border; his chancellor of instruction, Anthony Alvarado, had been superintendent of New York City's Community School District No. 2, where he had designed and launched a successful systemic instructional reform initiative. While Bersin managed the political, business, and organizational aspects of running the district, Alvarado attended to the instructional side of things—focusing on establishing a professional accountability system, concentrating all decision-making around issues of teaching quality, creating an infrastructure of reforms to improve the knowledge and skills of all personnel, and instituting a tightly coupled instructional-change process with a strong focus on equity as well as quality. Together, this pair sought to anchor the school system in research on teaching and learning. Their plan resulted in the creation of new and radically different learning opportunities, structures, and fiscal arrangements to support instruction across the district's network of schools. As Alvarado described the reform:

> The vision was to try to create an institutional focus on instruction that would begin to put into place the leadership, staff development, assessment, curricular supports that would be necessary to increase student achievement. That would actually begin to create the environment for a different kind of teaching that would generate both a narrower and more powerful set of student achievement results. So it's not just about raising reading scores. It's about changing the kind of teaching to get more challenging and thoughtful student work.

This effort has been a substantial undertaking. SDCS employs approximately 7,400 certificated teachers across nearly 180 schools, 18 of which are comprehensive high schools. As we describe in the chapters that follow, the effort encompassed virtually every aspect of district and school operations, from budgets and structures at the central office and district divisions to organizational culture and professional practice in individual schools and classrooms. And despite the fact that most of San Diego's students are low-income students of color with wide-ranging English language skills, achievement has increased in the city schools during these early years of the reform.

Organization of the Book

To focus our analysis of changes at the state, district, and local school levels, we treat three major kinds of policies that influence teaching and instruction: (1) curriculum and assessment initiatives, (2) teacher-development initiatives, and (3) accountability initiatives. We look at how these played out in different contexts and were influenced by agents at each level of the system.

In chapter 2 we more fully describe the San Diego City Schools' district reform initiatives, how district leaders redesigned the "top" of the system while also seeking to drive changes at the school level, and how San Diego has managed and leveraged state policy. Chapter 3 discusses early results of the reform, examining both trends in student achievement and changes in practice and school culture from the vantage point of various actors in the system. Chapter 4 examines the reform from the perspective of elementary schools, and chapter 5 does the same using cases of three San Diego middle schools as the focus for exploring how policies function differently in different school contexts. In chapter 6, we enter the classroom to follow the effects of the reform on three middle school teachers, whose experiences illustrate the ways in which efforts to transform teaching play out for teachers at different points in their careers and in different settings. Chapter 7 examines a reform of the original reform, emphasizing the district's new push for high school change. In this chapter we look at how district leaders need to be able to imagine and design an "ambidextrous" organization (Tushman & O'Reilly, 1996) that can sponsor innovation in areas where well-developed organizational forms are not adequate to evolving needs. In chapter 8, we conclude by revisiting the tensions—described earlier—between centralization and decentralization and between autonomy and professionalism, and we draw some lessons for leadership in the cause of improved teaching and learning.

NOTES

1. The principals' survey was sent to 180 schools; responses were received from 161 schools for a response rate of 89%. The teacher survey was sent to 581 teachers in 11 randomly selected schools and to an additional 114 teachers in our three case-study schools. The response rate for the random sample was 70%, and the response rate for the random sample plus case-study schools was 69%.

2. While the state intends for BTSA to reduce attrition among new teachers by providing them with support to improve their teaching, BTSA does not address the large numbers of teachers without full credentials currently in classrooms. Initially, districts used BTSA funds at their own discretion to support any novice teacher, regardless of her credential status. In 2001, the BTSA program began enforcing use of BTSA funds only for first- and second-year teachers with full credentials. In response, California expanded the intern programs and, more recently, the preintern programs to provide some support for underprepared teachers and to increase the likelihood that those teachers would complete their credentials and stay in the profession. Peer assistance and review (PAR) funds can also be used to support uncredentialed teachers, but this patchwork of initiatives does not reach all candidates in ways that are helpful to them (Shields et al., 2001).

CHAPTER 2

Instructional Reform in San Diego City Schools: A Thoughtful Strategy for Change

Quite often, schools have operated as though teachers come into the profession with all of the knowledge they need to teach—and in many times and places, this conception of knowledge has been quite thin, comprising a bit of content knowledge, the ability to stay ahead of the students in the textbook, and perhaps a smattering of generic teaching methods. The job of the school organization was to provide each teacher with a classroom and a set of books, and to make sure the other accoutrements of school—lunchtime, recess, field trips, PTA meetings, and the like—were set up around the edges of the self-managing classrooms. Teachers taught as they chose behind closed doors. Principals visited infrequently to check on whether order reigned and students appeared busy. Traditional expectations for schools did not include a set of strong ideas about the nature and quality of instruction or instructional improvement, or the role of school leaders in developing such instruction.

THE THEORY OF SAN DIEGO'S REFORM

Confronting and changing these traditional views of "doing school" and creating a well-grounded, *shared* set of instructional practices—built upon sophisticated pedagogical knowledge—was at the heart of San Diego's reform. Much of the intellectual momentum for these changes came with Tony Alvarado, who brought with him a well-developed theory of teaching and learning. This philosophy was grounded in a deep understanding of how children learn and the principles of effective instruction, as well as a clear theory of system change. At the center of his ideas about the change process were commitments to focused, intensive professional development and to the development of professional accountability, which together are designed to improve the knowledge and skills of educators and to create a press for good practice. These ideas evolved from his work in New York City's District No. 2 (for a description, see Elmore & Burney, 1999) and were further developed in collaboration with Alan Bersin in San Diego.

Starting with a Theory of Instruction

San Diego's instructional efforts were built on several decades of research by cognitive and developmental psychologists and other education researchers on learning and teaching (see, e.g., Bransford, Brown, & R. Cocking, 1999; Resnick, 1995; Resnick & Hall, 1998). This work emphasizes the importance of:

- setting clear goals and performance standards aimed at higher-order thinking skills and performance abilities;
- carefully assessing student learning by evaluating students' thinking, strategies, skills, and products and then scaffolding the learning process to ensure that students can achieve these goals; and
- using a mix of teaching strategies that explicitly model and demonstrate key skills, engage students in active production of meaningful work with opportunities for extensive practice and revision, provide multiple pathways for access to content, attend to students' prior knowledge and cultural experiences, and teach students to think metacognitively about their learning strategies.

The district developed a variety of strategies to disseminate this instructional knowledge base so that it could inform teaching across classrooms and drive district decisions about curriculum, instruction, assessment, and school organization. In designing teacher-development programs in both New York City and San Diego, Alvarado consulted researchers at the University of Pittsburgh's Learning Research and Development Center (LRDC), experts at other universities, and literacy specialists from Marie Clay's Reading Recovery Program.

A companion to this theory of learning is a theory of teaching that proceeds from the premise that student learning will increase when powerful interactions occur between students and teachers around challenging content. The expectation is that as teachers' efforts become more grounded in knowledge about effective instruction, their teaching practice will better support student learning. Since learning depends on extensive teacher knowledge of both individual learners and of teaching strategies, and since it requires diagnostic skill in figuring out how best to organize learning opportunities that meet learners' particular needs, this theory of teaching relies on the development of teacher expertise, rather than on the adoption of scripted or "teacher-proof" curriculum. A scripted approach, in contrast to an approach based on expertise, would constrain teachers from adopting strategies that address the individual needs of students, and thus undermine the effectiveness of teachers.

Alvarado and Bersin describe their instructional theory as an attempt to professionalize teaching by grounding decisions both in greater shared knowledge about effective practice and in an expectation that teachers will learn to apply knowledge to students' individual needs. This professional conception includes the notion that practice must be shared and become public so that all students can learn. Drawing parallels between the work of teachers, surgeons, and lawyers, Bersin observed in a talk to the district's high school principals:

> A professional draws on professional skill and knowledge to apply to the changing facts before her. Professionals deal with problems and solve problems based on applying a body of knowledge to a particular case. When we all look back—some of us 10 years from now, some 25—and say, "What was it that we were experiencing in the opening years of the 21st century in San Diego and then around the country?" I predict it will be the history of the professionalization of teachers and of the educational world, in the sense that teaching no longer is a private preserve. It is a public province of feedback, discussion, interaction, peer review, and constant improvement much more akin to the way in which traditional professions have operated but which has not operated in education. The notion that a classroom is a private preserve is a value that still exists in the world and is inconsistent with the professionalization of teaching. This does not mean that there is not creativity. In fact, that is the essence of the professional path: to exercise

discretion based on the facts of the problem before you and draw from all your training and skill and knowledge and apply it to the case to produce a successful result.

A key component of this press to professionalize teaching is the notion that, when powerful norms of practice exist, teachers are individually accountable for operating according to these norms and using the knowledge on which they are based. In teaching, professionalism has commonly been misunderstood as representing individual autonomy and control over one's own practice rather than a commitment to common norms of practice and methods for improving them. To develop this kind of widespread professional knowledge and skill, Alvarado and Bersin focused their attention especially on the professional development of teachers, principals, and other staff, on the assumption that structures and opportunities established by the larger district system can facilitate quality teaching.

Alvarado's and Bersin's beliefs about how to achieve this goal rested heavily on recent research about teacher learning. This research argues for the provision of professional development opportunities and networks that provide access to knowledge about pedagogical strategies that are productive for teaching *particular* kinds of content. Equally importantly, professional development supports continuous reflection and refinement of practice in communal settings that enable studying and discussing practice, as well as modeling and coaching within classrooms. These approaches allow teachers both to learn about practice *in* practice and to dislodge norms of private teaching practice (see, e.g., Ball & Cohen, 1999; Darling-Hammond, 1997a; Evans & Mohr, 1999; Fountas & Pinnell, 1996; Little, 1999; McLaughlin & Oberman, 1996). Creating such opportunities rests, in turn, on leadership that prioritizes teaching and learning; shared expectations and commitments that all students can learn to high standards; and teaching and learning standards that well represent the kinds of learning desired, are coherent in their expectations, and are tied to diagnostic assessment tools that can guide practice.

This theory of teaching and learning, combined with the belief that literacy is a gatekeeping skill undergirding all other kinds of learning, translated into a district-wide focus on literacy, intensive investments in the improvement of professional practice, and the development of accountability mechanisms for ensuring improvement among the lowest-performing students, schools, and employees. District leaders devised a series of instructional measures to focus district norms and culture directly on these priorities. We describe these below.

Proceeding with a Theory of Change

To infuse this instructional theory into district operations, district leaders followed a change process that was highly directive, prioritizing speed of implementation and fidelity to the instructional theory over mechanisms to solicit input and ensure backing about the changes underway from organizational members (Hightower, 2001). While allowing district leaders to root their system in common design principles, this strategy stood in contrast to incremental approaches (e.g., Lindblom, 1980) and ignored cautions about the importance of upfront "buy-in" from organizational members (McLaughlin & Oberman, 1996; Fullan, 1991, 1993). The San Diego leaders' theory of change centered around the belief that systemic, instructional reform in an entrenched district system had to begin with a "boom" or a "jolt"—including radical changes in many preexisting structures, cultures, and norms—before reforms and new support structures could take hold. As Bersin explained:

> There was no other way to start systemic reform. You don't announce it. You've got to jolt the system. I understood that. . . . If people don't understand you're serious about change in the first 6 months, the bureaucracy will own you. The bureaucracy will defeat you at every turn if you give it a chance.

The speed with which the reform program was designed and implemented was in large part a function of the political imperatives under which Bersin was hired. Following a teachers strike in 1996, community confidence in SDCS was low. Public perceptions that the district was too bureaucratic, was poorly preparing its students for college and work, and was moving too slowly on needed reforms led to a move by the local Business Roundtable to elect new board members. The new board discontinued the prior superintendent's contract in 1997 and hired Bersin in 1998 with a mandate for immediate change. The board was split 3-2 throughout most of Bersin's tenure, with the key three votes tied to support from the business community, which had strong vested interests in the system, not only because of concerns about the local economy, but also because many members sent their children to public schools in La Jolla and other affluent parts of the city. To keep this slim majority on his side, Bersin felt the need to act and show results quickly.

It is important to note that while the San Diego reform followed many of the strategies Alvarado had used in District No. 2 to improve instruction, the model of change was very different. District No. 2 took a much slower approach to reform, with the process extending over the course of a decade. Furthermore, many of the instructional ideas were already well known to a substantial cadre of teachers and were embedded in some of New York City's longstanding teacher-education and professional-development programs, which served as a support in preparing novices and supporting veterans in their practice and which had strong relationships with a number of local schools. Alvarado's many years of experience in the city as superintendent of two community school districts and as one-time chancellor of the Board of Education made him a well-known figure trusted by many reformers and by the teachers union, with whom he worked closely to develop innovative practices and school capacity. Many of the difficulties that were later encountered in communicating and implementing San Diego's reform—as well as some of the successes—can be traced to the speed with which this complicated and wrenching set of changes was undertaken, as well as to the changes themselves.

DEVELOPING PROFESSIONAL PRACTICE: THE GOAL OF REFORM

The core of the reform was the design and provision of an extensive array of professional-development opportunities for principals, teachers, and other district-wide leaders, which served as the key mechanism for spreading the theory of instruction across the district. New resource-allocation patterns, described in chapter 3, supported these opportunities, as well as the district's efforts to establish literacy as an important gatekeeping skill and to develop equity systems to close performance gaps and raise performance levels of the lowest achieving students.

Building an Infrastructure for Professional Development

By design, all professional development activities in SDCS have incorporated time and structures enabling teachers and principals to interact with peers and reflect about practice; they also have emphasized the role of continuous, context-specific learning networks. Within a couple of years, most professional-development opportunities were embedded in schools and classrooms. In order for organizational members to internalize the district's theory of instruction, these opportunities were designed to generate knowledge across the profession as opposed to impart information to individuals (see Hightower & McLaughlin, 2002).

Among the first, most fundamental instructional reforms instituted were mechanisms for *principals* to learn about how to develop and monitor high-quality teaching among their staffs. The district's 175 principals were divided into seven heterogeneous "learning communities," each of which was led by a newly promoted and trained central-office "instructional leader" (IL), who replaced the traditional assistant superintendent positions. Each IL was a former principal who had demonstrated high levels of understanding and skill as an instructional leader. Alvarado took these leaders to District No. 2 during the initial summer to observe schools and to participate in summer literacy activities so that they could lay a foundation for the work they would do with principals and teachers in San Diego.

The learning community groups convened during required, monthly principals' conferences, which offered principals opportunities to learn about leading school staffs in high-quality instructional practices. The format of the principals' conferences varied, including both interactive "field trips" to local classrooms and discussions with local and international experts on relevant topics (e.g., teaching techniques, the principal's role as instructional leader). Sometimes school- and central-office administrators jointly examined student performance data to focus attention on the lowest performers and means for increasing their learning. Principals also interacted individually with ILs through "walk-throughs," which are occasions when ILs visit a school to observe classroom practice, evaluate site progress, and assist principals in identifying specific instructional support needs. ILs visited each of their schools at least three times a year; some schools had visits as often as monthly.

San Diego's leaders invested in developing instructional knowledge among administrators because they believed that instructional alignment requires shared knowledge throughout the system about the technical core of the work. The goal is to enable decisions that support good teaching to be made with minimum dissonance. Furthermore, if principals are to serve as instructional leaders, they must know instruction well. The change model assumes that individuals in key positions across the system—both within schools and in the central office—are needed to introduce and sustain instructional reform within classrooms. Through a variety of professional knowledge-building efforts, the larger district system became more equipped to facilitate professional development within and across school communities. As we describe later, principals became more competent on-site leaders, better able to help teachers incorporate professional learning into their everyday routines as a community of learners within their school, and better able to evaluate the quality of classroom teaching.

The district also worked intensively on strengthening the professional development of *teachers*. During summers and intersessions, SDCS offered extensive professional-development workshops—including about 150 classes each year—that ranged in length from 1 to 7 days. Most classes were held on school campuses, and participants received $15 per hour to attend. At least once a year, principals received lists of their teachers who had attended particular district workshops. These lists helped the principals to keep tabs on the teachers' exposure to ideas and to better calibrate the level of knowledge about instructional strategies among the staffs. Beginning in year three, the district combined these training opportunities with the provision of summer school classes for students performing below grade level. During these classes—which, on most campuses, were taught by a subset of the school's regular teaching staff—teachers had opportunities to view demonstration lessons taught by experts and to practice techniques with experienced coaches working by their side. These workshops were intended to mesh with ongoing within-school professional development activities, as teachers met with principals, peers, and school-based coaches to discuss instructional matters.

Indeed, a key part of the professional development for teachers was the development of a *network* of trained and certified *peer coaches/staff developers*, who were placed in schools to work directly with classroom teachers on teaching practice. The district intended for coaches to reinforce the district's literacy strategy and theory of instruction within the context of each school site, and to break down norms of private practice. The district arranged for coaches in elementary schools to work with new teachers on induction, in addition to coaching other teachers who were receptive to support. Those at the secondary level worked primarily with English teachers; in secondary schools, induction was handled separately. By year two, at least one half-time coach had been placed in two-thirds of district schools; by year three, all schools had at least one full-time peer coach/staff developer. Coaches accomplished teachers who had been identified by principals and expressed interest in this position—were university certified and trained by literacy staff from the district. They worked in schools and classrooms 4 days a week. On the fifth day, coaches trained with their peers and district literacy experts. Staff developers spoke very highly of this training, and through it were able to form important professional relationships that gave them a means to reflect on their roles and circulate curriculum and pedagogical strategies.

In a survey of teachers conducted for this study during 2001, 96% of respondents reported attending professional-development workshops, conferences, or training, and 75% reported engaging in regularly scheduled collaboration with other teachers on issues of instruction. These professional-development opportunities for teachers were designed to help make teaching public and to parallel research about instruction, which argues for focusing on "authentic tasks," "long-term assistance," and communal activities (Stein & D'Amico, 2002).

Focusing on Literacy

District leaders contended that literacy holds a special place in the learning process: improved literacy skills not only influence test scores (not surprisingly, students generally do better on tests they can read than on those they cannot), they also provide the key to access higher-level content in other areas. For this reason, the teaching of literacy provides an important, common initial learning agenda for adults as they begin to function in learning communities (Elmore & Burney, 1999) and learn to "speak a common language" about instructional practice. Thus, from the beginning and across all grade levels, literacy instruction was a privileged skill in which teachers were trained and around which professional development activities were oriented. During the 2001 school year, more than 93% of teachers we surveyed reported having attended professional-development activities that focused on language arts or reading, and 79% had attended more than eight hours of such activities, noticeably more than any other category. Furthermore, teachers reported this training to be more useful than any other category of professional development: 69% rated the training's usefulness at three or above on a five-point Likert Scale, and a large majority of elementary teachers rated it "very useful."

The district's reading strategy was grounded in a balanced literacy approach that includes emphasis on decoding skills and phonemic awareness alongside equal emphasis on comprehension and expression through participation in language-rich listening and speaking activities, reading of trade books and other materials, and extensive writing. The Literacy Framework supporting these activities outlines specific teaching techniques to improve students' literacy skills. This framework is grounded on research on literacy learning and teaching; this research appears in the district's training efforts through literature that translates research into practice. For example, faculty used such works as: Irene C. Fountas and Gay Su Pinnell's *Guided Reading: Good First Teaching for All Children* (1996) and *Word Matters* (1998); Anne Cunningham and Keith Stanovich's *What Reading Does for the Mind* (1998); Janet Allen and Kyle Gonzalez's *There's Room for Me Here: Literacy Workshop in the Middle School* (1998); works by Janine Batzel on balanced reading and by Ro Griffiths and Faye Bolton on guided reading.

The Literacy Framework includes certain pedagogical teaching components, such as read-alouds, independent reading, word study, observation and assessment, shared and guided reading, and modeled, shared, guided, and independent writing (see Stein & D'Amico, 2002). These strategies translate into such practices as the use of word walls and classroom displays of exemplary student work tied to specific standards, as well as close assessment of student skills through running records, miscue analyses, and other diagnostic tools. Supported by specialized professional-development activities, district administrators expect principals and teachers to become knowledgeable about each component of the Literacy Framework and to move in stages toward its full implementation.

Alvarado emphasized that this was a professional reform, not a hierarchical reform—that the authority for the frameworks and teaching strategies is the research base on which they rest, not the say-so of the central office, as is often the case with centralized curriculum initiatives:

> We've organized into frameworks what the profession knows about instructional work. It is the profession that is [the source of] the expectations, not the district. When you speak and work with [your staff], they have to understand this is coming as a function of the profession, not as a function of the district demanding it. If an outside force is focusing me to do something, then I'm an automaton. If I'm responsible for using professional knowledge, then I have a big role in accessing that knowledge and implementing it. You only have a profession when there is a common set of knowledge and procedures that guides the work of the professionals in it. The idea of what good professionals do is access that [common practice and knowledge base] and continue to learn about its application in a particular context. The parts that are in there are driven by professional knowledge, not because four people consult and invent it. You're being driven by the canons, knowledge and skill of the profession, [and this is] a function of professional practice.

Communicating the sources of the reform and enabling principals and teachers to understand deeply the knowledge undergirding the initiative was a major challenge that took all of the nearly 5 years in which we observed the reform process and that was still ongoing when the research concluded. For reasons of both tradition and implementation, the reform was often perceived, especially in the first years, as hierarchical, rather than professional.

The reform initially emphasized literacy as the primary focus of elementary schooling, especially in the earliest grades. By the third year, the district had added a mathematics focus. To support the literacy focus at the secondary level, the district instituted a set of courses called "Genre Studies"[1] as a way to bolster students' reading comprehension and writing skills. The district adopted a set of local diagnostic assessments to assess students' reading levels and, if needed, to place them in Genre Studies classes. All sixth graders and high school students reading below their grade level were required to take these two-hour classes, which were designed as accelerated rather than remedial classes. The instructional leaders pressured principals to assign their best teachers to teach Genre Studies courses. The courses were taught at reduced class sizes, and the district channeled extra funds to schools in proportion to the number of students demonstrating a need for these courses.

Local Accountability: Student Equity and Teacher Professionalism

San Diego's local reforms took place in the context of the state's high-stakes, student outcome-oriented accountability policies, and state tests certainly had the attention of district leaders, principals, and teachers. However, unlike the state-level accountability approach, which was predicated on a theory that rewards and sanctions would supply the motivation for raising test scores, San Diego's approach saw the problem as a need for greater professional knowledge and greater investments in struggling students, rather than merely a need for greater motivation. The district's conception of accountability sought to strengthen performance and reduce inequities by improving the quality of teaching received by all students, especially those with the greatest educational needs. District reformers' goals for increasing "equity" were defined operationally as increasing the performance of all students, moving the bottom quartiles up, and reducing the gap between high and low performers. The district monitored "quality" in terms of the percentage of students in the lowest quartiles, arguing that "by lifting the floor we also are raising the ceiling."

The conception of accountability embedded in San Diego's theory of change is tightly tied to notions of *professional* accountability, that is, accountability of professional staff for the quality of the teaching and schooling practices in which they are engaged and for continual improvements in their professional knowledge and skill (Darling-Hammond, 1997b). This kind of accountability requires educators to take responsibility for self and peer learning and for engaging in discourse around instructional practice. Specifically, teachers are responsible for using, both individually and collectively within their schools, teaching strategies that reflect professional standards of practice, and for engaging in professional development. Principals and peer coaches are responsible for developing the teaching in their schools and for supporting teachers' learning. Through structured learning communities, principals are accountable to one another for peer and self-learning about how to lead staff development, and for a commitment to reduce inequitable student learning opportunities.

Professional accountability as a demand on principals, coaches, and teachers rests on a notion of reciprocal accountability within the system (Elmore, 2000). In a context of reciprocal accountability, leaders are responsible for developing conditions that will enable individual and collective learning; it is this learning for which teachers, principals, and district leaders are held accountable in return. As Elmore (2000) notes, a district system that is geared toward professional learning is predicated on distributed leadership, wherein each level of the system is concerned with the core function—instruction and its improvement—but operates within its bounds of "comparative advantage." The district takes responsibility for providing the necessary supports for professionals to succeed in changing their practices to become successful with all students. Thus, in San Diego, all principals participated in learning communities, and all schools received classroom-based professional development from peer coaches, while all teachers were expected to engage in professional development, coaching, and collaboration.

Furthermore, the district invested disproportionately in the lowest-performing schools to facilitate their climb in closing the gap. In addition to providing continuous, high-quality professional development to aid teachers in raising the quality of instruction in every classroom, the district supported the lowest-performing students through more focused curricula (e.g., Genre Studies), extended instructional time (summer school and after-school instruction), and parent contracts. The eight lowest performing schools ("focus schools," determined by the state Academic Performance Index) received an additional full-time peer coach, 24 more instructional days each year, enhanced parent training and involvement programs, four mathematics specialists who would work directly with students, and programs for preschoolers. First-grade teachers in these schools received $8,000 each for purchasing enhanced materials ($3,000 more than first-grade teachers at other schools). The district also identified 11 other low-performing elementary schools, which received an additional full-time peer coach and increased per-classroom allocations for enhanced first-grade materials. In short, the district invested heavily in organizational structures that leaders hoped would foster professional accountability across principals and among faculties within schools.

Reforming Personnel Policies: Getting and Keeping the Best

A reform built around professional expertise requires major rethinking of how professionals are recruited, supported, and evaluated. To build resources for hiring and training high-quality teachers, the district reexamined staffing patterns and recruitment strategies, simultaneously increasing the incentives to become fully prepared before entering the classroom. As we describe further in chapter 3, in order to hire a greater number of trained teachers and to lower pupil-to-teacher ratios, the system decreased the number of central-office personnel, project administrators, and paraprofessionals. The personnel office, under the leadership of a new human resources administrator, Deberie Gomez, began to recruit aggressively for well-trained teachers. The recruitment techniques included collaborating with universities on new training programs in high-need fields and creating smooth pathways with local schools of education; offering contracts to well-prepared teachers as early as possible, sometimes as much as a year in advance of teaching; and reaching out to well-prepared teachers in other states.

In addition, Gomez streamlined the hiring process, put the entire system online, and improved the system's capacity to manage data, interviews, and other components of the selection system that, when poorly managed, had slowed the process and caused many candidates to give up on the system and go elsewhere. In fields with particularly severe shortages, such as special education and bilingual education, the district began to work with local universities to create and operate teacher-education programs.

Great progress was made over the 3 years from 1998 to 2001 as a function of aggressive recruitment, collaboration, and overhauling of the personnel system, making it possible and expected for all schools to be staffed by trained teachers. The percentage of SDCS teachers who were less than fully credentialed was less than 5% in 2000–2001 (CDE, 2001e), compared to a statewide average of 14% (Shields et al., 2001) and an average in some other cities of well over 20%. By fall 2001, while districts like San Francisco and Los Angeles hired hundreds of teachers on emergency permits, and more than 50% of the state's newly hired beginning teachers lacked full credentials, San Diego filled almost all of its 1,081 vacancies with credentialed teachers. Through purposeful action over several years of efforts to improve the teaching force, when school opened that year, the district had filled all but two special education positions, and it had eliminated all but 17 emergency permits and waivers.[2]

The district also worked to create a professional-accountability system that intensified the supervision and development of principals and teachers and led to counseling out or dismissing those who were unable to meet more rigorous standards for performance. Many districts feel they cannot insist on high performance from personnel during times of shortage, because they are not sure they can find replacements. San Diego's strategy has been to increase incentives to ensure that qualified teachers are hired and to focus unremittingly on both supporting and evaluating the quality of practice. A number of beginning teachers we interviewed confessed that they had sought out San Diego rather than other districts because they felt the quality of professional development they would receive would surpass what they could experience elsewhere, and they were enticed by the challenge of developing cutting-edge practice.

While the district focused attention on developing the practices of teachers and site administrators, it also was willing to weed out ineffective or unnecessary employees from both the central office and the schools. Principals worked closely with the district's human resources office in documenting extremely low-performing teachers in order to pave the way for their ultimate dismissal from the district. Instructional leaders reassigned to the classroom a number of principals who had not demonstrated effective instructional leadership on-site. At the end of the first year of the reform (1999), 15 site administrators were reassigned to classrooms for failure to demonstrate effective instructional leadership. By the end of the second year of the reform, about 30 of the district's principals (15% of the total) were counseled out of their leadership positions (Hightower, 2001). To enact a reform based on professionalizing teaching, the district needed to attend to all of the policies and practices that influence the caliber of the professional workforce, including hiring and retaining individuals who are professionally skilled, as well as building supports for their ongoing learning.

FORGING COHERENT DISTRICT STRATEGY: MEDIATING STATE POLICIES

To accomplish its goals, San Diego needed not only to develop its own reform initiatives, but it also needed to manage and respond to those emanating from the state. From the perspective of an outside agent such as the state, we might say that the district's primary reform strategies comprise the foundation that external policies must penetrate to have any effect on the district's activities. From an inside-out perspective, we might say that the district's strategies must contend with state and other external policy interventions and conditions that may either impede or support the reform initiatives. Below we examine how district leaders in San Diego leveraged, mediated, and sometimes side-stepped state policies in order to maintain internal coherence and to further the instructional improvement goals of the district.

Three key examples from San Diego City Schools' reform strategy illustrate the district's active management of the broader state context as state-initiated policies hit the ground in San Diego. We explore how the state's teacher-development policies, reading initiative, and accountability measures interacted with San Diego's district-wide strategy for on-site, teacher-driven professional development, strongly articulated vision of balanced literacy, and disproportionate investment in the lowest performing students and schools.

District Professional Learning:
Leveraging State Teacher-Quality Policies

While state policies were developed essentially to apply emergency-room triage in the face of the large proportion of underprepared teachers and their concentration in high-poverty schools, San Diego placed itself in a position to work on improving professional skill for all teachers. In addition to creating a well-designed set of recruitment, preparation, and retention efforts, the district took advantage of recent state incentives supporting teacher recruitment to help achieve this goal. These actions included productive use of state funding for hard-to-staff schools through the Teachers as a Priority program—recruiting initiatives that took advantage of subsidies such as forgivable scholarships and loans for teacher-education candidates who would teach in high-need schools— and state-funded internship programs that San Diego City Schools designed with nearby universities to meet the demand for bilingual and special education teachers.

San Diego also leveraged the well-funded state Beginning Teacher Support and Assessment (BTSA) program to serve its reform initiative, parlaying state BTSA funds to augment the on-site peer-coaching infrastructure for literacy that had already been established at the elementary level. The decision to subsume BTSA activities into the activities of literacy peer coaches in elementary schools is an example of the district's effort to create coherence across policies. New teachers mentored through BTSA received the same substantive messages about the district's theory of teaching and learning as their peers throughout the school, while being coached in ways appropriate for their development as novice teachers. Because new elementary teachers were integrated into the overall reform initiative of the district, their students were exposed to the same balanced literacy approach as students in the classrooms of more experienced teachers. Furthermore, San Diego's beginning teachers received the opportunity to learn content-specific pedagogy for literacy instruction, which extended beyond the generic approach to teaching supported by the state-sponsored assessment of teaching used in BTSA.[3] Finally, by using BTSA funds to support new teachers' work under the elementary literacy-reform umbrella, San Diego resisted fragmenting the focus of teachers, peer coaches, and district leaders. Within the literacy initiative at the elementary level, the district did not conceive of BTSA as a separate, disparate program as many other districts might have.

Districts can also ignore or marginalize external policies to protect their own reform agendas, as San Diego did with the state Peer Assistance and Review (PAR) program. In the late 1990s, California replaced the popular California Mentor Teacher Program with the PAR program, which focuses on peer assessment and review of underperforming veteran teachers and can also support mentoring of novice teachers to supplement BTSA. The enabling legislation mandated that PAR must be negotiated locally between each school board and its district bargaining unit. In the context of a highly acrimonious relationship between the district and the local teachers union, San Diego PAR became a separate and more marginal program, providing funds at the school level for the support of mentors who assisted teachers on request and discretionary funds for professional-development supports not provided by the district's literacy initiative. District use of both the BTSA and PAR programs—in the case of BTSA, aimed at integration, and in the case of PAR, at maintaining a distance from the reform—attempted to protect the coherence of the literacy initiative in San Diego.

Despite the inevitable difficulties in implementing new programs like BTSA and PAR, San Diego was well ahead of many other districts in its efforts to ensure that beginning teachers received mentoring. Statewide, only 39% of first- and second-year teachers participated in BTSA in 2001, and a smaller number participated in other support programs, including PAR. A statewide teacher survey in that year found that 70% of beginning teachers reported being assigned a mentor, but fewer than one-third received regular coaching from assigned mentors (Shields et al., 2001). In San Diego, 86% of teachers hired between 1998 and 2001 (a pool that included experienced teachers transferring from other districts) reported having a formally assigned mentor during their first and/or second year of teaching, and 54% saw their mentor at least monthly for classroom observations and/or discussions about their teaching. This compares to 47% of beginning teachers in BTSA and 16% of other beginning teachers statewide (Shields et al., 2001, p. 102).

The State's Reading Initiative

The ways in which San Diego's leaders mediated and leveraged aspects of the California Reading Initiative to support their own balanced literacy approach is a lesson in strategic opportunism anchored in a theory of instruction and of change.[4] The approach to balanced literacy in San Diego, as embodied in its Literacy Framework, is arguably richer than the state's vision of literacy as embodied in the state standards, framework, and current assessments. San Diego's Literacy Framework, grounded in research on teaching and learning, encompasses a broad array of pedagogical strategies and expected outcomes from students, including extensive, high-level strategic reading and writing; evidence-based discussion and other forms of oral discourse emphasizing reasoning and expression; and basic decoding and comprehension.

The carefully developed Literacy Framework has served as an anchor against the pendulum swings in state reading policies—from "basic skills" to "whole language" to "phonics" and back again. The specificity of the framework and the purposefulness of the district's strategy allowed San Diego to take advantage of the funds available for training related to the state's components of literacy to support the portions of teachers' learning that map onto the state's goals (e.g., the teaching of phonemic awareness and decoding skills). The district's other professional-development work extended beyond the state reading initiative using the multiple components of the Literacy Framework. Throughout the period of our research, San Diego was able to keep the richness of its balanced literacy approach and maintain the breadth and depth of literacy training the district believed its teachers needed.

The State Accountability Scheme

San Diego schools were, of course, subject to the same accountability rules as other districts in the state. It is worth noting that the state's approach largely skirted districts and rested heavily on the schools themselves, which were rewarded and sanctioned based on their performances. This approach could easily cause a rift between district- and school-reform directions, and it did in many districts. Particularly with regard to the Immediate Intervention/Underperforming Schools Program (II/USP), teachers and principals could be torn between the recommendations of the evaluator and district initiatives. Attempting to preempt this potential conflict, San Diego City Schools acted on behalf of all of its 42 II/USP schools in selecting one firm as the external evaluator for all of the schools and negotiating the approach of the evaluator to ensure that it would be consistent with the district's theory of instruction. District administrators strongly believed that the lowest-performing schools were the very ones that most needed to keep their focus on literacy and that the district's literacy approach would prove successful for students who were at risk of not reading. Rather than allow the schools to spin off on potentially disparate paths, the district worked to subsume this state policy into its overall reform initiative.

Although the state accountability policies were designed to circumvent districts in many ways, in San Diego the role of the district was instrumental in mediating a largely punitive accountability approach and transforming it into one that was based on professional support and an explicit priority on equity in student learning. Rather than managing testing pressures by holding back large numbers of students so that their scores would look better, or pushing out those with low scores to special education or GED programs to improve the average, SDCS's blueprint specified multiple strategies for investing heavily in low-performing schools and low-performing students so that both would have real opportunities to improve. Not only did this orientation recognize that building capacity in the lowest-performing schools required much more investment than at high-performing schools, but the investment was also undergirded by a coherent theory of instruction and professional development aimed at helping traditionally underserved students learn. In this sense, the district actually focused and sharpened state policy to develop a more rational performance-based accountability system than what the state itself had enacted.

To further mitigate the punitive nature of the state's accountability measures, the district intervened on behalf of the schools that were under threat of state takeover. It proactively developed a plan for those schools, gave them additional human and fiscal resources, and won a waiver from the state for a self-monitoring effort. To the extent that the plan reflected the district's main reform initiatives, this effort again kept schools from falling out of step with the district's theory of instruction. In mediating state policies in these ways, San Diego had some advantages not available to some other districts. First, its reduction in emergency permit teachers allowed it to use its BTSA funds to better advantage. (BTSA could not be used for emergency credentialed teachers.) Second, because of its size and its purposeful management, San Diego was able to use state professional-development funds to meet its own needs. These advantages, coupled with its strategic approach, allowed San Diego to manage the state's initiatives and use state resources to further its instructional goals.

NOTES

1. "Genre Studies" courses were later renamed Literacy Block courses and then two-hour or three-hour Readers'/Writers' Workshop courses.

2. In 2000–2001, the district had a total of 403 teachers working on emergency permits and six working on credential waivers, as well as 149 on intern or preintern credentials, according to the California Commission on Teacher Credentialing (CCTC, 2003). In 2001–2002, among 9,369 professional staff, the district records showed only 15 working on emergency permits and two working on credential waivers (about one tenth of 1%). This sharp reduction in emergency credentialed teachers was in part a function of recent reforms that increased recruiting power and aimed to support and retain qualified teachers. In addition, San Diego moved many underprepared teachers previously working on emergency permits into more structured programs. In 2001–2002, district records showed 182 teachers working as interns and 204 as preinterns—individuals who are teaching while in training. Including all of these classifications, the proportion of underqualified teachers working in San Diego totaled only 4.3% as compared to about 25% in Los Angeles, for example. The share of underqualified teachers decreased by 28% between 2001 and 2002 as the size of the teaching force grew (San Diego personnel records, tabulations, July 2, 2002).

3. The state-sponsored formative assessment, California Formative Assessment and Support System for Teachers (CFASST), is not required of districts, but most districts use it in lieu of developing their own materials that would have to be approved by the state.

4. No claims can be made about relationships between the state's development of its reading initiative and the development of the balanced literacy initiative in San Diego. The initiatives developed on different tracks with different time frames and under different immediate influences.

CHAPTER 3

Changing the System at the Top: Rethinking the District

Much reform in U.S. schools has been an add-on enterprise. Although many change initiatives begin with a focus on how schools should change, few have considered how central-office operations, district resource allocations, and management structures must also change to support a major redesign of educational work. As San Diego City Schools mobilized itself to focus on quality instruction in all of its schools for all of its students, Superintendent Bersin and Chancellor Alvarado sought to embed this charge in every aspect of their operations—from the central office to the classroom and everywhere in between.

The "jolts" to the system occurred in both instructional and operational domains. While much attention has been placed primarily on the instructional sphere, it is important to review how the district's fiscal policies and organizational structures were changed radically to enable implementation of the reform (Hightower, 2001, 2002a). Changes occurred in terms of resource allocations, organizational structures, and personnel policies needed to focus on the development of expert teaching.

REALLOCATING RESOURCES

Rather than subscribing to a typical district expenditure pattern whereby resources maintain the status quo (Guthrie & Sanders, 2001; Meyer, Scott, & Strang, 1994; Miles & Guiney, 2000), San Diego leaders sought to have instructional priorities drive resource acquisition and allocation in SDCS. All funds coming into the district—including local funds, such as resources from foundations and those identified through internal cost-saving measures, federal monies such as Title I, and funds connected to such state policies as teacher induction and accountability— were redirected to finance the instructional strategies devised to serve the district's theory of teaching and learning. The goal was to focus on improving the core technology of schools—the quality of teaching—and to invest in high-functioning classrooms rather than peripheral programs. Alan Bersin described the importance of using resource reallocation as a lever for developing both focus and capacity within a school system:

> We had a *plan*. We had a design. We had a purpose. And we allocated as far as we could to meet the capacity of the system to absorb the change so that, for example, it was always a question of "here are a whole series of things we want to do" and we would bring funding up to meet them as far as they did. Now along the way there were obviously choices that had to be made about just what was going to be reallocated in what year. But by and large we were always ahead of the capacity of the system to supply the talent sufficient to really make it work. The constraints here were *capacity*, in some ways, as much as money. In those years when there was considerable new money coming into the system we were able to use that, together with reallocating significant resources from the prevailing resource base.

Having a plan and a design for the use of resources constituted a major change in standard operating procedures. Staff in the central office described the previous process in which funds entered the district for a variety of projects, and budgets were developed to fund many different ideas for marginal improvements. Project leaders, principals, and others in the central office would come to the budget office with various programmatic ideas and the financial staff would try to gather money to fund them. A high degree of local school autonomy and the ability of previous administrations to attract outside grants combined to produce a dizzying array of funded activities. One district administrator observed, "We were very highly regarded by foundations and cutting-edge stuff around the country, so we had a lot of projects" (Hightower, 2001, p. 18). These programs contributed to a large central office, which some viewed as fragmented, bureaucratic, and "top heavy," with one administrator for every ten teachers. A financial officer noted, "In San Diego, over the 20 years prior to the blueprint, we just received really tremendous amounts of money that basically didn't show a lot of results."

The change in approach was described by Karen Bachofer, who headed the new Standards and Assessment division:

> When we began this work it was clear that we decided that we were going to start with what was needed, what the Blueprint would be—not to start with how much money we had. And that's a dramatic change from how we'd done business in the past. Before, we'd say, "Well, we've got this much money; so what can we do?" This said, "What program do we need for the students?" And then we worked to find the money to fund the program, rather than the other way around.
>
> In the 15 years prior to this, I've never seen any kind of give-and-take. . . . Usually it was sort of like people going to the financial folks and saying, "We need to do this. Do you think you can find x-number of dollars?" And it was never a *dynamic* process. And it was never transparent. So it was clear to us: if we were going to do this, we would have to make some decisions about what we would and would not do. We had to prioritize what we would not do and make decisions about what we weren't going to do based on the efficacy of *that work*—not whether or not [the chief financial officer] could find an extra pot of dollars somewhere. . . . And we talked in depth to the budget people. It was very much a give-and-take situation: "You say you want to do this, and it's going to cost that, and here's something else you say you want to do. Now which of these do you think is going to get more return for the students? Which do you think is going to be more viable? Which do you think is going to make the whole thing more coherent?" So we had to make some choices about what we were going to keep, based on how much money the budget people were able to free up and to find.

Several hundred small and large categorical programs that proliferated over many decades because of federal, state, and local initiatives—most of which operated independently—were consolidated to serve core system needs for professional development and teaching improvement, or they were discontinued. Local funding was leveraged to support these efforts as well. The results of previously disconnected, widely varying philanthropic inputs were abandoned in order to adopt a focused use of foundation funding to support instructional priorities. This strategy had its trade-offs, however, as some funding opportunities were declined if they did not coincide with district priorities. For example, the district initially lost a grant from the National Science Foundation because the early reform efforts did not focus on math and science. The $6 million grant was later reinstated, but only after the district had executed its plan to prioritize an investment in literacy before it moved on to math and science.

Two years into the district's reform initiative, the SDCS school board passed a major policy package called the "Blueprint for Student Success in a Standards Based System," which codified the new uses of funds. In 2000–2001, about $61 million (6% of the district budget) was spent to support the "Blueprint" strategies, including peer coach/staff developers, extended day programs, summer/intercession programs, Literacy/Math Framework development and implementation, summer institutes for teachers, and leadership academies for site administrators. Nearly all of this money ($59 million) went to school sites. Nearly two-thirds of the funding for these initiatives came from Title I funds and integration program funds. Other federal and state funds, including a large segment from state-funded "hourly programs" that could be used to lengthen students' school day and year, accounted for nearly all of the remainder (see Figure 3.1).

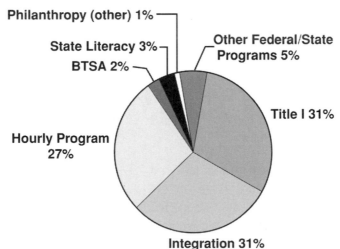

Figure 3.1. *"Blueprint" Funding (2000–2001). Budgeted Amount $61 Million.*

In 2001–2002, the district funded the "Blueprint" at a level of $91 million (9% of the district budget), using a similar strategy for consolidating federal and state funds, plus a larger share of foundation funding (see Figure 3.2). Again, nearly all of these funds ($88 million) went directly to schools. In the following year, the "Blueprint" funds increased once again, to $111 million.

These funds were allocated in a way that increased funding to schools, especially those serving the neediest students, but substantially decreased school-level autonomy in the use of these resources. Chief Administrative Officer Henry Hurley described how "approximately 80% of the money went directly into services that fit into the Blueprint strategies, and then there was a small amount left over, the 20%, that the school had discretion over how to spend."

Although schools surrendered most of the discretionary authority of their instructional programs to the central office, no schools received less than their predetermined categorical funding allocations, and most schools often received more funding as a part of their "Blueprint" funding package. Equally important was the message of solidarity that the "Blueprint" strategies communicated to school sites as to the purpose and direction of the district's efforts. As one elementary school

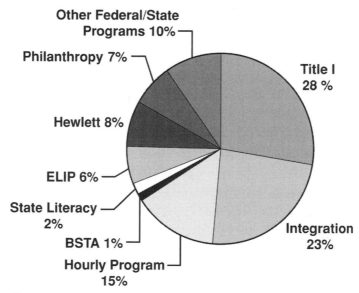

Figure 3.2. *"Blueprint" Funding (2001–2002). Budgeted Amount $91 Million.*

principal reflected on the process of adjusting to the reallocation of site-based funding:

> I had $600,000 redirected out of my site budget that I no longer have control over that went to the Blueprint. I'm having another about $300,000 [redirected] this year. I'm losing my Reading Recovery teachers to some other [assignments] where the people are going to go. . . . Now while I say "losing," I have to say I know exactly where it's going. . . . It's being distributed across our district so that we can bring up the bottom of every one of our children. . . . Do I believe in it across the district? Absolutely. Did it mean that I lost a whole bunch of discretionary money? Yeah.

While schools had less discretion in the use of the "Blueprint" funds, the central office was substantially reduced in size so that more resources could be sent to the school level. Bersin's tenure had begun with a promise to reduce central-office spending by 5%. In 1999, under order from the Board of Education, Bersin led a task force that began an extensive inventory of the district's central offices with a clear purpose "to restructure functions in the central office and to identify human resources and financial resources for redistribution to school sites."

In the first year of the reform, 112 jobs were eliminated from the central office, while only 10 were added. Each central-office employee was asked to respond to the question, "How do you support teaching and learning in the classroom?" Those whose responsibilities did not directly address this priority found their positions terminated. These displaced employees were either shifted to other roles in the district deemed essential in support of student learning or were discontinued. During the period 1999–2002, 282 positions and $11.6 million in central-office expenditures were eliminated and redistributed to school sites. A large part of these reductions freed up dollars to fund the substantial staffing requirements set out in the "Blueprint." These reductions also marked a clear revolution in the culture of how the central office viewed its role in supporting student achievement.

An additional major reallocation of resources occurred with the subtraction of over 600 of the district's 2,800 instructional aides in

2000–2001, with the savings invested in teachers and peer coach/staff developers—a trade of less-skilled for more-skilled personnel. Although it drew on a relatively small share of the total budget, this decision signaled a larger trend in redirecting district spending. During 2000–2001, overall district personnel expenditures increased by 10%, and spending on teachers increased by 12%, alongside a 19% *decrease* in spending on instructional aides (see Figure 3.3). While instructional-aide budgets dropped, the budgets for site administrators, teachers, and other school-site professionals all increased.

Playing a major role in this funding decision was the fact that district leaders found no research linking the work of instructional aides to the quality of instruction of the teachers they assisted and the

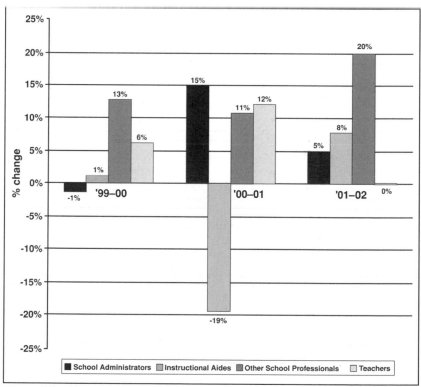

Figure 3.3. *Personnel Budget Trends.*

performance of the students they supported. Bersin described the rationale:

> The only systematic decision that was made was . . . that the 650 instructional aides that were in the system, for whom there was very little research support for the notion that they added much value to instruction, were typically the people who bore the brunt. What was interesting was that during a period of relative economic prosperity, every one of those folks was offered a full-time job to replace the lost employment. The large majority of them did not want the full-time employment, but rather preferred two to four hours near their home at the site. So we clearly had an example here in San Diego of what I think is typical across the nation in Title I, which is that somehow—and this is not to denigrate the efforts of instructional aides—it's that somehow Title I became an employment program *not* an instructional program.

Decisions such as these reflect a signature strategy behind the decision-making of SDCS leadership—investing and shifting resources toward educational strategies that have proven to be effective. These moves created substantial political resistance, including large protests at the board meeting where the budget including massive reductions in instructional aides was voted on. Bersin commented in 2002:

> [T]he tumult that came in terms of the implementation of the Blueprint was actually energizing resources and reallocating resources away from existing arrangements and existing programs to fund a new approach to improving student achievement. . . . In places where you move resources and you take jobs away from people you get the pushback that's going to be natural from that group of people who are affected by the change. . . . So it's not "we're doing this and we're going to throw a few new resources at it and have the Blueprint." You're actually taking employment arrangements and you're disrupting them in favor of a new approach. So it's not "well, we wish we could have all gotten along better." This is what a revolution is!

An examination of district budget spending over time indicates the broad impact the SDCS reform had on overall resource and funding allocations across the district. Not only did the introduction of the "Blueprint" impact the direct reallocation of resources and dollars to the plan's specific components, but the theory of change behind the "Blueprint" also influenced decisions about spending beyond the discrete elements of the reform package, as it was leveraged to create change on a broader scale. Trends in nonpersonnel spending offer a clear example of this phenomenon. Over the period of 1998–2002, with the introduction of the "Blueprint," nonpersonnel expenditures increased an average of 12% per year to underwrite specific investments needed for the materials to support the reform, including collections of leveled trade books in elementary and middle school classrooms and the hiring of peer coaches and other consultants to support within-school professional development. During this period, the average budgets for books/supplies for students and instructional consultants saw a substantial increase (27% and 24% respectively) while expenditures for travel/conferences for professional development *decreased* on average by 3%, as an infrastructure for teacher learning was developed within the district. Rather than incremental across-the-board increases (and during budget cuts, decreases) in budgetary line items that inherently preserve the status quo, the budgetary changes reflected the increased investment in on-site professional development resources (consultants, institutes for teachers, books and materials, etc.).

REDESIGNING THE CENTRAL OFFICE

The organization of the central office and its approach to supporting schools also changed substantially as part of the reform. In 1996–1997, the SDCS organization chart included seven divisions reporting to the superintendent; only two of these divisions were responsible for educational functions. Five area superintendents, each supervising a set of cluster leaders, oversaw the work of schools (see Figure 3.4). Hired with a mandate for leading substantial change, Bersin and Alvarado thought that the district's central office was fragmented, unfocused, and likely overstaffed. The district had roughly 50 major programs operating under the deputy superintendent in the district office. These programs, which included School-to-Career, Alternative Education, Curriculum Development, Healthy Start, and Summer School, operated independently and targeted the schools that fell within their scope across all five subdistricts. Assessing the district office's prior organization, Alvarado commented:

> There [were] no common organizing themes about what good teaching is, [or] what might good curriculum be, [or] what are some research-based supports. . . . So my view was that [the district] was fractionalized, that it was not coherent, that different parts of the system were sending different messages, [and] that there was an over-abundance of work to be done so that a million policies had gone on . . . and people were doing everything [only] an inch deep.

Rethinking the Organization

The evolution of the district organizational structure reveals a successive reorganization that has been guided by internal self-examination. Central to these efforts have been the questions: Have these resources

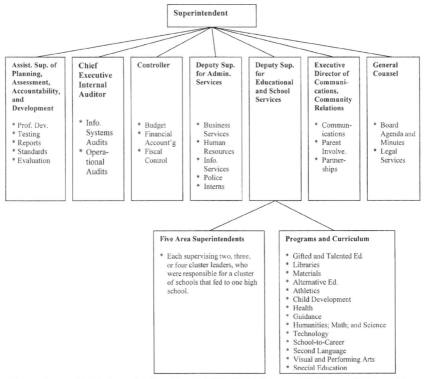

Figure 3.4.   *SDCS Organization Chart, 1996–1997.* Source: *Hightower, 2001, p. 12.*

been successful in supporting student learning? If not, what changes are needed to see that they do? Convinced that form must follow function, the district leadership has redesigned aspects of the organization every year to address needs that emerge.

Upon taking office, Bersin immediately "jolted" the district office by reorganizing it into three divisions that gave more prominence to the educational functions: the Institute for Learning; Administrative and Operational Support; and the Center for Collaborative Activities (see Figure 3.5). Alvarado led the Institute for Learning, which focused on curriculum, teaching strategies, and the professional development of teachers and

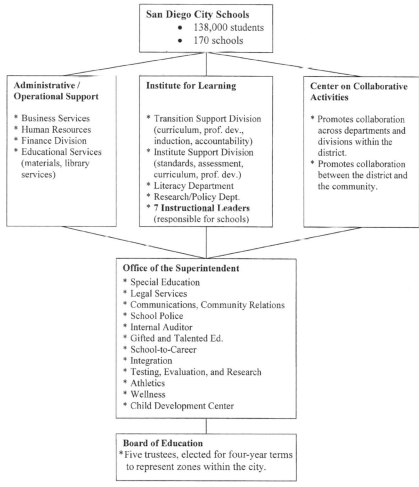

Figure 3.5. *SDCS Organization Chart, Fall 1998.* Source: *Hightower, 2001, p. 128.*

principals. It included the instructional leaders who replaced the five area superintendents. Administrative and Operational Support included business services and operational departments, and the Center for Collaborative Activities was a much smaller division, designed to facilitate collaboration among departments and programs. These major changes marked a radical departure from both the decentralized approach and the management by geographic area that were reflected in the five areas. Creating a leaner, more functional organization created waves, of course, but as Bersin noted later, "I was hired to be an agent of change and not a caretaker."

The composition of these divisions and the scope of their contributions evolved further in subsequent years. This evolution was influenced largely by a deepening of the organization's philosophy to establish quality instruction and student educational support as its first priority. In April 2000, the central office was reorganized a second time, eliminating positions again and creating a new department, the Center for Student Support and Special Education (CSSSE), to "transform the work of staff who support teaching and learning while providing interventions to meet the complex needs of students and families" and to "marshal and mobilize district and community resources to support students and families" (Report of the San Diego School Board, March 9, 2000 [see Figure 3.6]). The district had had difficulty managing special education, was under a court order, and wanted to gather funding to concentrate on the needs of struggling students. This division was able to focus the district's efforts to solve a number of problems that had not been addressed for years. Later the CSSSE was absorbed into the Institute for Learning, as further restructuring occurred in subsequent years.

More recently, the district organizational structure for the 2002–2003 school year illustrated the district's commitment to ongoing examination of its work and structure. Comprised of four major branches—Office of the Superintendent, Institute for Learning, Business Operations, and Facilities—the 2002–2003 district makeup was the result of continual fine-tuning and self-assessment. Refinements in the institute, for example, recognized the need for improved communication and efficiency in its service to schools. With a focus on streamlining functions and identifying senior managers, the institute was restructured by eliminating the 27 manager positions reporting to Alvarado and replacing them with five senior managers heading five major divisions of work (Student Services,

Figure 3.6. *SDCS Organization Chart, Summer 2000. *Librarians, counselors, mental health, etc.* Source: *Hightower, 2001, p. 241.*

Special Education, School Supervision/Support, Standards/Assessment, and Curriculum/Instruction). Not only was this reorganization a sound strategy toward resolving the bottleneck dilemma found within the chain of command, but it also enabled the institute to better execute its projects by organizing around major work groups.

Promoting Greater Efficiency and Effectiveness

While early changes to the organization focused especially on staffing arrangements and position shifts, changes in later years emphasized such nonstaff considerations as business systems and technology, with an eye toward improving the administrative performance of the system. In the June 25, 2002, Board Report, Bersin declared, "The proposed organizational structure contained in this document creates a foundation that begins a customer-focused organization." Following this charge, district initiatives invested greater resources in business and technology systems that would improve central-administration efficiency, while also improving services to school sites and easing the administrative burden on school-site administrators.

In 2002 the district launched its District Wide Application (DWA) initiative to replace the aging and inefficient business systems of SDCS with an integrated and improved student information system, human resources system, and financial system. DWA was a large-scale initiative that included upgrades to the district's IT infrastructure, increased network capacity, improved technology support, and comprehensive staff training. The initiative sought to create uniform business systems across the district that would ease the administrative burden on school sites through better central services, as well as provide significant returns on investment as costs and wasted resources were reduced through increased efficiency in operations. SDCS Chief Business Officer Ronne Froman commented on the need to have the reform touch every aspect of the organization:

> [Y]ou know, we've been talking about business reform, and what's become perfectly clear to me now, over the last few months, is that it's truly all education reform. . . . I can't really separate them. They're all so intertwined. . . . [The district leadership] focused first on teaching and learning and what we're doing now is we're building the mold or the infrastructure to be able to cradle the teaching and learning. And so it's all part of one thing. And I keep talking about this: it's like a cobweb or a net that connects the whole entire district. And you really can't talk about one without talking about another.

A necessary offshoot to the district's focus on improved central operations was the implementation of a revamped budget system for central-office departments and school sites. Abandoning status quo procedures of the past in which annual budgets were a simple carbon copy of previous years' budgets—with minor revisions for salary adjustments—the district adopted a "zero-based" budget system in which annual budgets for departments and schools were based on projections stemming from historical spending patterns and planned activities for the future. A more focused district agenda influenced a more intentional strategy for planning and budgeting dollars. Jeff Wiemann, deputy chief of SDCS business operations, explained the new process:

> What we would do on a zero-based budget review is go out and have everybody review their budgets, review their actual spending patterns over the last couple of years and plan if they see any major changes in the future and work hand in hand to establish that budget. So by redirecting, we're going to be capturing some of those site funds and make sure they're spending them on first what they need to be buying and potentially going to a blueprint model.

Shifts in the methodology and procedures for budget planning also resulted in a necessary redesign of the role and structure of the central budget office. With a desire to improve customer service to schools, the district office reassigned its budget analysts so that each school could work with only one person, thus improving communication between the central office and school sites. As described by Wiemann:

> If I'm a principal at a school site, up until [2002], I would have to go to five, six, seven different budget analysts to get a true picture of my budget at my school. And that's because the budget analysts were arranged by fund code. I could be in a poverty area and I could have twenty different categorical funds and that could cause me to go to five or six or seven budget analysts. So we worked and realigned all the budget analysts so that each school was assigned one budget analyst. So they manage schools instead of funds. So that was really the first major step. So now going forward we would be able to have the budget analyst sit down with whomever the principal wants from the school and with a couple of people from our department to be able to walk them through that.

The ultimate goal in increasing the efficiency of central-office procedures and systems is to promote and support school-site leadership, so that principals no longer have to worry about cumbersome budget procedures and can instead devote more time to the classroom and supporting instruction. Developing intelligent support structures is the goal of a redesign that gave budget officials direct responsibility and commitment to the well-being of education in the specific schools they serve. As Wiemann explained:

> A key component is holding people accountable for their budgets. Part of our instructional reform has principals spending more time in the class-room and so we from the business side are trying to give them more tools and processes to be able to simplify the operations management at the school site. So what we're looking at right now is how do we remake the site management for our principal? How can we deliver goods and ser-vices to the school site and how can we basically put the support struc-ture for our principal? And so what we want to be able to do is to put a support structure in place that they basically have one phone number that they need to call. In the past, the principal would call and get a voicemail and not get responded to for a couple of days. So we're creating basically a call center where they can call and they're going to have somebody there to be their action person that's going to help them solve the problem.

The strategies evolution of the SDCS organizational structure illus-trates the commitment of its leaders to creating an organization that re-mains firm in its focus, yet fluid in its structure, in order to adjust to and meet organizational demands.

A COMMITMENT TO ONGOING REFORM

Critical to the success of the SDCS reform effort has been a leadership that insists that the mission of the work must shape the structures and functions of the organization. As needs shifted, so did the leadership's strategies and structures for implementation and execution. This same philosophy has continued. During the early half of 2003, as the district announced plans for the 2003–2004 budget, Superintendent Bersin surprised many by proposing a 50/50 split between the central office and schools with respect to discretionary authority over the $36 mil-lion in Title I funds coming into the district. Acknowledging the progress of teachers and principals in developing their knowledge of best practices in instruction and learning, Bersin concluded that the best use of those dollars would be to give school sites more autonomy in making spending decisions. This departure from the 80/20 split strategy practiced in previous years reflected the policy employed by the district since the reform began in 1998—responsive decision-making driven by a commitment to improving instruction and service to students.

Even more noteworthy was the district's ability to maintain this commitment in light of the California state budget crisis in 2002 and 2003. Faced with $148 million in total projected budget cuts, SDCS leaders devised a plan to reduce the 2003–2004 "Blueprint" budget by $36 million (approximately 33%) while still maintaining the program's focus on addressing the evolving needs of the students. As stated by Chief Academic Officer Mary Hopper in a May 13, 2003, report to the Board of Education, "Although the current fiscal crisis forced modifications to the *Blueprint*, staff worked to ensure that the integrity of the plan remains intact." To accomplish this, the district sought to adhere to the core purpose of each "Blueprint" strategy, and then made adjustments—deciding which programs to conclude, continue, expand, and/or implement—based on careful monitoring and assessment of what was going on in schools.

For example, funding for materials to enhance classrooms for literacy development in elementary schools was discontinued, not because of a heavy price tag but because after 3 years of implementation it was concluded that the original purpose of this strategy had been accomplished: every K–6 classroom in the district had been provided with materials to support the literacy program. These dollars were freed up in part to meet the necessary budget cuts, but a portion was also redirected to meet an emerging need for increased resources and training for science instruction in high schools. Other decisions rested on a need to set priorities in times of funding restraints. For example, such services as extended day and summer school offerings were scaled back at high-performing schools (those scoring at the 7th through 10th deciles on the state's Academic Performance Index) while every school in the district scoring in the first two deciles on the API received more support than the previous year (peer coach/staff developers, resource teachers, etc.). In this case, a decision was made to recapture dollars while also redirecting funding to support the district's neediest students

and schools. In times of budget cuts and funding restraints it is tempt-
ing to apply a strategy of blanket percentage cuts and staff terminations
across an organization, but the case of San Diego City Schools illustrates how strategic planning can guide these decisions more productively. An early investment in setting a vision, strategy, and plan for the
work of the organization and its reform provided SDCS leaders with a
barometer and basis for making informed decisions based on preestab-
lished priorities, goals, and assessments. Such a strategy aims to enable
the SDCS administration to continue to effectively address the evolving needs, demands, and capacity of its organization while maintaining
its mission to "improve student achievement by supporting teaching
and learning in the classroom."

CHAPTER 4

Charting the Results of the Reform

The effort to turn any large system in a new direction is rather like redirecting a gigantic ocean liner: it takes considerable energy, time, and consistent pressure on the rudder of the vessel to overcome the momentum of the previous course and undertake a new route. The outcomes of these efforts are not immediately apparent in the indicators usually observed by the public, but begin with changes in norms and more widely shared practices, eventually appearing in other measures, such as students' engagement and performance in school. All reforms have costs as well as benefits, and it is important for leaders to be able to understand and weigh the trade-offs. Furthermore, change always engenders conflict, which can be both productive and destructive in terms of the relationships and practices that are negotiated and renegotiated as norms and policies shift. In this chapter, we look at the results of San Diego's efforts in all of these areas, aiming to provide a realistic look at what this approach to systemic reform entailed and how it impacted students, educators, individual schools, and the system as a whole.

IMPROVEMENTS IN STUDENT ACHIEVEMENT

San Diego witnessed substantial increases on the state assessments after the reform's inception; district leaders viewed these increases in student performance as validating the reform underway. The proportions of students scoring above the 50th percentile on the SAT-9 tests increased from 41% to 48% in reading and from 45% to 54% in mathematics between

1998 and 2002 (see Appendix A). Furthermore, gains were most dramatic in the grade levels specifically targeted by particular aspects of the reforms: the early elementary grades and middle school literacy. For example, over these 4 years the proportion of second graders scoring above the 50th percentile in reading increased from 43% to 61% and in mathematics from 50% to 64%. While scores increased statewide during this period, neither average scores nor participation rates increased as steeply as in San Diego, especially at the elementary level (Quick et al., 2003). Furthermore, San Diego's student body includes a much larger proportion of low-income students and students of color than the state as a whole. (The district student population is 75% "minority," 60% of its students are free- and reduced-price lunch participants, and 30% are designated as limited-English proficient.)

Importantly, gains in average scores and in the proportions of students scoring above the 50th percentile occurred while the number of students taking the test also increased substantially. Participation rates grew by more than 20% on both the reading and mathematics tests between 1998 and 2001. In most schools, more than 98% of students were participating in the tests by 2001. District scores sometimes rise as more low-scoring students are held out of the test, are moved into non-tested programs (e.g., special education), or are counseled to leave school for GED programs or other alternatives. Conversely, average scores tend to decline as low-achieving students are added to the testing pool. This appears not to have been the case in San Diego. Scores continued to increase in 2001, when there were large increases in the test-participation rates of English learners and other students who were not previously tested.

A sizeable number and proportion of students moved from the lowest two quartiles to the upper two quartiles in both reading and math between 1998 and 2001, especially in the early grades where the literacy initiatives have most consistently taken root. For example, the proportion of students scoring in the bottom quartile in reading dropped from 36% in 1998 to 29% in 2001, while the proportion scoring in the top quartile increased from 20% to 24%. Based on 4 years of SAT-9 data, 7,800 more "Q1-2 students" (students initially scoring in the bottom two quartiles) scored above the 50th percentile in reading in 2001 than in 1998, and over 9,000 more "Q1-2 students" scored above the

50th percentile in mathematics.[1] Increases occurred across all grade
levels but were much larger at the elementary and middle levels than at
the high school level, especially in reading, where high school students
performed noticeably worse than younger students. As we discuss later,
secondary school achievement was the focus of a new high school initiative undertaken by the district in 2001.

CHANGES WITHIN THE CENTRAL OFFICE

Within the central office, budget and operations managers learned to
collaborate with instructional administrators to specify and prioritize
educational needs and to direct district dollars toward instructional priorities. Both instructional and operational administrators commented
on a shift *away* from letting the available money guide program and
policy decisions and *toward* having district-wide, articulated, instructional needs govern the budget. Alvarado described the shift as getting
"operational departments [to] become the handmaiden of instruction,"
noting that the reform:

> created a group of people working together for the first time in which the
> . . . instructional issues drove [decisions], and the budget people and the
> operational people knew that their job was to make the budget thing hap-
> pen. That's a *very* important thing to happen in districts. It almost never
> happens.

As we described in chapter 3, substantial shifts in the allocations of
funds occurred, enabling much larger investments in professional development, teacher recruitment, mentoring, coaching, and other factors that
supported the district's efforts to hire, support, and develop well-qualified
teachers who were well-supported in their learning and teaching.

There were also short-term costs to these focused changes. The district initially lost its National Science Foundation grant because the
"Blueprint" focus did not include math and science in the first year. The
$6 million grant was later reinstated, and the district also secured a $3
million grant from the Foundation for the Improvement of Mathematics and Science. Central-office capacity in mathematics was initially reduced until a new person was hired to lead the district's math division,

and the Mathematics Framework guiding new investments in curriculum and professional development was approved by the board in 2000. Science support also languished until new curriculum initiatives were launched in 2001. Special education was left out of the reform until 2001, when efforts to bring the district into compliance and to build capacity brought it under the wing of the Institute for Learning and led to the placement of 49 site-based diagnostic resource teachers to support this function in schools.

The prioritization of instruction over operations also had short-term costs, as it was more difficult to attract attention to repairs and other noninstructional items in the early years of the reform. Over time this imbalance, too, was redressed. Instructional leaders described how their roles evolved over the first 3 years of the reform, as they gradually took on more aspects of instruction and, ultimately, operations as well, reincorporating aspects of the former assistant superintendent roles. As one noted:

> When we first started we were almost exclusively focused on instruction—and exclusively on literacy. Over the course of the 3 years we moved into math and took on other operational issues, first with a focus on the second language program and special education, then the school budgets, to the point now where we're clearly responsible, through the principal, for whatever happens at the school. Although we don't get into a lot of details on operational issues, if there's a crisis or a particular issue, then we're expected to step in and help to solve it, and it seems like that echoes back more to what the assistant superintendent's role was prior to the reorganization.

The expansion of the instructional leaders' job was not, however, a return to the status quo, because, in contrast to earlier years, these instructional leaders were chosen for their deep knowledge of teaching and learning, were assisted in learning how to oversee and develop instructional programs and support principals as instructional leaders, and were held accountable for improving instruction. Thus, as they assumed other functions of the previous organizational roles, they did so with a different foundation of knowledge, with new structures in place to support schools and the change process, and with a new mandate.

SCHOOL-LEVEL REACTIONS

As we noted earlier, leadership in a context of reciprocal accountability is not intended to be a zero-sum power game in which different role incumbents win or lose control under varying governance schemes. Instead, the combination of complementary strengths should enable strong roles for district personnel, school leaders, and teachers. However, the process of developing a sense of shared accountability can be uncomfortable in an organization that has not previously experienced a strong press for focus and results. Our survey data, collected during the second and third years of the reform (2000–2001), indicate that principal and teacher reactions to the reforms exhibited both an appreciation for new supports and, not surprisingly, some discomfort with changes in norms of practice.

Principal Reactions

Principals were mostly pleased about the district-initiated changes, but were also wary of the increased scrutiny of their work. More than 75% of those surveyed felt that the district "holds high expectations and is committed to high standards," "holds priorities consistent with those of the school," "helps the school focus on and nurture teaching and learning," and "promotes principal and teacher development."[2] The widespread enthusiasm was expressed by this principal after the first year of the reform:

> It's very exciting [to hear conversations at] the staff meetings and grade level meetings [at our school], or just conversations in the teachers' lounge . . . the very different questions for the reflections they have, or the conversations around curriculum or instruction. It's really quite amazing to see the change in teachers.

At the same time, just over half of principals (55%) said that they saw the district as centralized and hierarchical, creating mandates without providing adequate support. This sentiment was strongest among high school principals. Only 56% felt that "the district inspires the best in job performance."[3] Nonetheless, more than two-thirds of principals at each level felt that "the district supports my school's efforts to improve."

The commitment of principals initially skeptical to the reform tended to rise over time, as their deeper understanding of the reform's intentions increased with greater communication. Many grew more supportive as they saw how the professional development available to themselves and teachers enabled them to develop stronger practice. In many cases, a view of the reform as hierarchically imposed shifted as the professional basis for the work became clearer. One principal described her own evolution this way:

> I resisted Alvarado because I don't like being told what to do, and who knows better than I do, for crying out loud! So there was resentment there. But I think [Alvarado] is sincere, and I think he's got a very simple plan, but it makes a lot of sense: focus on good teaching; support good teaching, and learning will come. And he's absolutely right. . . . And so I shared with [my staff], "We're going to do this, this, and this," and they said, "Why?" And I said, "Because we're being told to do it, that's why." Because I didn't get the "why" either, and there were missing pieces. Information came out piece by piece. We had this attitude of we'll be saluting and we'll do it. Then when I finally heard Alvarado talk to the middle-level principals in a forum where he just talked to us, I came back here and said to the staff, "I need to tell you that I've finally heard the whole plan, the whole picture, what it's about, and each and every one of us would be happy to be chancellor and mandate this if we could. . . . It makes absolute sense." It's common sense; it's a good thing. Who doesn't want a kid who will read and write in grades 8 and 9 because we've addressed it in grade 7? So they agreed with me.

The vast majority of principals we interviewed (approximately 40) recognized the structural supports for their learning. They appreciated their instructional leaders, liked the Learning Community groupings, and noted the monthly principals' conferences as a source of professional growth and inspiration as well as an important conduit for information between schools and the central office. They viewed walk-throughs—a practice in which principals and instructional leaders walk through the school and stop to assess teaching in each of the classrooms—as positive, non-threatening opportunities to interact with the IL on a more personal, context-specific basis. One principal noted that the IL model made the district more responsible for teaching quality:

> There's a sense that they [the instructional leaders] really know what's going on at our schools, where I didn't really feel that as tightly in the old model. So it feels like the *system* is becoming more accountable. Each piece is making the whole organization more accountable.

In addition, a majority of principals spoke favorably about the reform's "equalizing" quality and its focus on helping principals gain access to professional knowledge. They noted that everyone—not just specific schools or areas of town—was gaining access to comparable information about effective teaching and learning strategies. One veteran elementary school principal explained:

> It strikes me that the clusters were totally dependent on the vision of their leader, the Assistant Superintendent. So each cluster lived or died by that individual's futuristic goal or vision about education. Now, that doesn't exist. Our immediate Instructional Leaders gets the vision from the top; we all hear the same thing . . . the same message. And that consistency helps me to know that when I look at someone who's on the other side of town, they're trying to do the same thing I'm trying to do. And that's very reassuring, rather than to think: "Gosh, they've got the corner on the market for something I haven't even heard about." At least we're all in the same sailboat.

These perceptions are corroborated by survey data of principals (see Table 4.1). More than 90% cited as valuable the school- and district-sponsored staff development, instructional leader school visitations, the district's focus on low-achieving students, and the three-hour Literacy Block. However, elementary principals valued supports like the principals' Learning Communities, the monthly principal conferences, and the discussions with other principals and institute staff much more than secondary principals did. Elementary principals valued reform strategies that most impacted their schools, like the developmental reading assessment. Meanwhile, secondary principals highly valued the Genre Studies courses, which were implemented in grades 6–12, affecting most middle and high schools.

Table 4.1.   Principals' Views of San Diego Reforms (2000–2001)

% Rating Item Highly Valuable or Positive[1]	Overall (n = 180)	Elementary School	Middle School	High School
School-sponsored staff development	99%	99%	100%	100%
Institute-sponsored staff development	96%	99%	91%	87%
District's focus on Q1-Q2 students	94%	95%	86%	93%
Instructional leader school visitations	92%	94%	91%	80%
Discussions with my instructional leader	92%	93%	91%	80%
Three-hour Literacy Block	92%	98%	66%	60%
Principals' Learning Communities	88%	96%	69%	54%
Discussions with my school staff developer	85%	80%	100%	100%
Developmental reading assessment (used in elementary schools)	84%	90%	58%	33%
Genre Studies course (used in grades 6–12)	83%	57%	100%	84%
Monthly principals' conferences	83%	89%	70%	46%
Discussions with principals in my Learning Community	81%	93%	50%	46%
Portfolio assessments	60%	66%	53%	23%
Discussions with institute (district) staff other than instructional leader	58%	66%	32%	27%

[1]Percent responding 4 or 5 on a 5-point Likert Scale where "5" is extremely valuable, or responding 3 or 4 on a 4-point Likert Scale where "4" means very positive. *Source:* CTP Principal Survey, May 2000.

Overall, the survey data showed that a large majority of principals at each level felt that the district supported their school reform efforts. However, a sizable minority of secondary school principals (39%) felt that the district did not *understand* their school's reform agenda, a response echoed by only about 5% of elementary and middle school principals. One major bone of contention was that the initial focus on literacy appeared to ignore subject-matter distinctions at the high school level. As one high school principal commented: "[W]hen Bersin says that literacy is going to be . . . the only game in town, it's *not* . . . at the senior high school. At the other [level]s, it *can* be the only game. But at senior high, it's only going to be a piece of it" (Hightower, 2001, p. 42).

In the initial years of San Diego's district-wide reform, leaders intentionally pursued a system-wide strategy with little differentiation by grade level or subject matter. "Learning Communities," the district's variation on clusters established in 1998, were heterogeneously grouped by geography and school level. While Alvarado recognized the potential value of grade-level groupings, he feared that creating such groups would minimize "the K–12 thinking that has to go on" (Hightower, 2001, p. 137). Increasingly, however, high school principals bristled at the apparent "one size fits all" approach. They felt that district reformers lacked knowledge related to the particular needs of high schools and that the K–12 instructional conferences largely failed to meet their learning needs.

In response to these sentiments, district leaders decided to reorganize the Learning Communities to create two high school-only groups. Following board approval, Bersin and Alvarado announced this restructuring at a principals' conference in fall 2000. In making this change, however, they underscored that it was not a retreat from K–12 thinking; rather, it was an attempt to respond to the expressed needs of high schools. As Bersin explained:

> High schools, in fact, require not separate treatment but *different* treatment. There is a [grade-level] difference, and we have to take it into account. . . . Without cutting ourselves adrift from our [K–8] colleagues and understanding that what happens in the elementary school is absolutely critical to the success of our students in high school, we also will confront the fact that high schools require their own approach. (Hightower, 2001, p. 248)

This change represented an important recognition by the district that, in the context of system-wide reform, high schools may require reform strategies specific to their level.

While the survey data reveal general trends in the principals' perceptions of the reform, they do not fully reflect the concerns principals shared in one-on-one interviews or meetings. In addition to the secondary school tensions, principals often lamented a lack of support for noninstructional or "operational" matters. While appreciating the renewed central-office support for instruction, some administrators felt that a day or more off-site each month for principals' conferences created tension between on-site responsibilities and their own professional learning. Principals also spoke about feeling overworked and somewhat fearful

about the pressures and consequences for principal and school performance under the new district administration.

One of the main tensions under a system of reciprocal accountability is
balancing a focus on high performance with adequate supports. Principals
often talked about the high stakes attached to the role of the principal—a
reality driven home by the fact that a number of site administrators had
been moved out of their jobs in the first 2 years of the reform. Prior to the
Bersin administration, principals rarely were removed from their schools
other than through voluntary transfers. In extreme cases, questionable
principals were placed in central-office roles. Accordingly, the new personnel actions came as a shock, particularly to site administrators, many
of whom wondered about their own job stability. Still, the principals who
remained largely supported the intentions of the reforms and expressed
the view that improvements were tangible.

Teacher Reactions

Teachers' reactions to the district's instructional reforms were much
more mixed. In general, the teachers voiced appreciation for the district's emphasis on professional development and improving instruction; however, many disagreed with the implementation of the reform
initiatives, claiming the process was "too cut-throat" (from an elementary teacher), "top-down" (from an elementary teacher), and "bureaucratic" (from a Genre Studies high school teacher).

Elementary school teachers appeared more comfortable with the reform principles and literacy focus than were middle or high school
teachers, who raised questions about the literacy initiative's relevance
for all teachers, schools, and students. A common theme, also raised in
a recent American Institutes for Research study of the San Diego reforms (AIR, 2003), was that most teachers agreed with the goals and
substance of the reform agenda, but many felt discomfort with centralized implementation that seemed not to take their views into account.
Their responses illustrate some of the challenges associated with a
large-scale reform strategy that hinges on establishing common norms
of practice that defy the traditional individualistic culture of schools.
The responses also reveal some of the perceived trade-offs among competing uses of time and resources in the reform strategy.

Views of Professional Leadership and Support

Consistent with the district's goal of providing supports to enable teachers to be successful in what they are held accountable for—professional learning—most teachers had positive perceptions of their principals' instructional leadership and of their own opportunities for professional development. A majority of teachers surveyed saw their principals as leaders in school reform who set high standards for teaching and for student achievement (82%), and who maintained a strong focus on student learning within the school (68%). More than three-quarters also reported that their principals were involved in professional development with teachers (see Table 4.2). These responses represent an unusually high vote of confidence in local school principals. However, reflecting a sense of centralized decision-making, a minority of teachers (38%) said their principal was strongly committed to shared decision-making. These comments suggest that collegial work was focused more on professional learning than participatory governance.

Teachers also reported engaging in substantial amounts of professional development, with 96% having engaged in some kind of workshop or other training and 25% having offered professional development to colleagues. Whereas a minority of a national sample of teachers reported spending more than eight hours in professional development activities on any topic in 1999 (National Center for Education Statistics, 1999), most

Table 4.2. Teachers' Views of Principal Leadership

Proportion of Teachers Agreeing[1] That:	All Teachers (n = 404)	Elementary School	Middle School	High School
The principal sets high standards for teaching	82%	89%	70%	61%
The principal participates in professional-development activities with teachers	77%	84%	69%	60%
The principal ensures that student learning is the "bottom line" in the school	68%	79%	60%	50%
The principal is a strong leader in school reform	62%	67%	54%	60%
The principal is strongly committed to shared decision-making	38%	41%	36%	30%

[1]Percentage responding 4 or 5 on a 5-point Likert Scale where 5 is "strongly agree." *Source:* CTP Teacher Survey, Spring 2001.

San Diego teachers reported spending more than eight hours in professional development regarding reading (79%), methods of teaching (62%), and new curriculum and instructional materials (54%).

That teaching was becoming more public was also reflected in the fact that 75% of San Diego teachers engaged in regularly scheduled collaboration with other teachers, and 61% participated in mentoring or peer coaching. More than half (57%) participated in observations in other schools (see Table 4.3). Within their own schools, observations were even more frequent: 82% of teachers reported that they had observed another teacher teaching, and 75% reported that they had been observed by another teacher at least several times a year. Teachers reported further substantive collaboration on a regular basis (i.e., at least once a month), such as working together to develop curriculum materials or activities for particular classes (60%), discussing lessons that were not particularly successful (54%), teaching with a colleague (33%), and analyzing student work with other teachers (39%). Embedding professional learning into the everyday activities of a school is far more difficult than mounting formal professional development activities. Half of San Diego teachers surveyed agreed with the statement, "Our stance toward our work is one of inquiry and reflection." This average, however, reflected the positive responses of 60% of elementary teachers as compared to fewer than 40% of secondary teachers.

Table 4.3. **Teacher Participation in Professional Development**

Types of Professional Development Engaged in the Last 12 Months:	All Teachers	Elementary School	Middle School	High School
Attending workshops, conferences, or training	96%	98%	92%	93%
Regularly scheduled collaboration with other teachers on instructional issues	75%	83%	63%	69%
Mentoring or peer observation/ coaching	61%	70%	56%	41%
Observational visits to other schools	57%	64%	56%	34%
Presenting at workshops or conferences	25%	25%	24%	33%
Individual or collaborative research	55%	58%	49%	60%
University courses (beyond initial certification courses)	30%	30%	35%	33%
Participating in a teacher network	27%	24%	26%	34%

San Diego teachers' views of their formal professional development experiences were, on the whole, more favorable than averages found in recent statewide studies of California teachers (see Shields et al., 1999 and 2001). Nearly two-thirds of those surveyed agreed that the professional development they engaged in presented new information, increased their knowledge of instructional and assessment techniques in their teaching field, increased their effectiveness with students, and deepened their subject-matter knowledge. Once again there was a divide between elementary and secondary teachers: About three-quarters of elementary teachers agreed with these statements as compared to about half of secondary teachers. Approximately half of all teachers felt that they improved their skills for working with a diverse student population and for identifying instructional goals appropriate for their subject matter. Approximately half also felt that the professional development they experienced motivated them to seek additional learning opportunities; this was true for 61% of elementary teachers but only 36% of high school teachers (see Table 4.4).

Table 4.4.   Teachers' Views of Professional Development

Effects of Professional-Development Participation:[1]	All Teachers (n=404)	Elementary School	Middle School	High School
Provided information that was new to me	66%	77%	58%	50%
Increased my knowledge beyond basic instructional and assessment techniques appropriate for my subject matter	64%	73%	58%	50%
Increased my effectiveness at promoting student learning	64%	72%	58%	56%
Deepened my grasp of subject matter	63%	76%	58%	45%
Improved my skills to meet instructional needs of a diverse student population	52%	59%	53%	50%
Improved my ability to identify instructional goals appropriate to the subject matter I taught	52%	63%	53%	47%
Caused me to seek further information or training	52%	61%	45%	36%

[1]Percent of teachers replying 3 or 4 ("somewhat" or "a lot") on a 4-point Likert Scale. *Source:* CTP Teacher Survey, Spring 2001.

Beginning teachers seemed especially enthusiastic about the training they received and about the creation of school-wide practices. As one noted:

> For me, being a newer teacher, this has been great. The first 2 years I taught, I felt really lost. . . . I'm here, brand new, trying to create every-thing myself. . . . It was really stressful and really difficult. And so when the District came in and said, "here this is what you're supposed to do" and I started getting some training. . . . All of these things for me have been great! I'm finally given some direction. Everybody's doing the same thing. And I'm feeling more in touch with everybody else.

Consonant with these generally positive views about their professional learning, San Diego teachers expressed optimism about their ability to influence student learning. Large majorities agreed that "by trying different teaching methods, I can significantly affect my students' achievement" (81%), and 67% reported that their expectations for their students' learning had been increasing. Comparable proportions disagreed with statements suggesting that their "students cannot learn the material they are supposed to be taught" (68% disagreed) or that there is "little I can do to insure that most of my students achieve at a high level" (80% disagreed). Many teachers—particularly in elementary grades and the Genre Studies courses at secondary level—offered examples of how the reform had changed and deepened their own practice and how they were incorporating many of the strategies in their classrooms. We describe these changes in later chapters.

Views of the School Environment

Most teachers also felt that their colleagues were providing a high quality of instruction and were committed to improving student learning. Their views were more divided as to whether the emphasis on standards translated into coherent curriculum plans that are relevant to all students and consistent across grade levels and classrooms. Middle school teachers reported the least confidence about the coherence and clarity of their school's curriculum and standards. Across the board, relatively few teachers (30%) reported that they had enough resources for their work (see Table 4.5).

Table 4.5.   Teachers' Views of Their School Environment

Proportion of Teachers Agreeing[1] That:	All Teachers	Elementary School	Middle School	High School
The school staff is committed to helping students learn	89%	91%	88%	86%
Teachers provide high-quality instruction	88%	90%	81%	78%
This school has high standards for students' academic performance	70%	77%	53%	65%
This school has well-defined learning expectations for all students	59%	67%	40%	63%
Students are well aware of the learning expectations of this school	57%	62%	50%	59%
Standards for student achievement are challenging, attainable, and measurable	56%	64%	43%	55%
Our stance toward our work is one of inquiry and reflection	51%	60%	38%	39%
This school has high-quality school-wide curriculum plans	50%	55%	33%	57%
This school has consistent standards from classroom to classroom	45%	57%	25%	28%
The curriculum is relevant for the population of students	37%	45%	26%	39%
Resources are distributed equitably within this school	37%	45%	29%	24%
The curriculum is planned between and among grades to promote continuity	32%	36%	21%	36%
The resources available to me are sufficient for me to do my job	30%	27%	38%	29%

[1]Percentage responding 4 or 5 on a 5-point Likert Scale where 5 is "strongly agree."

In interviews, teachers voiced concerns about: (1) a lack of curriculum materials to accompany the literacy focus; (2) the homogeneous tracking of lowest performers into Genre Studies, a practice that appeared to contradict some research on learning; and (3) lack of attention to subject areas beyond literacy. Some also complained that as resources were pulled in different directions, the reform had eliminated school-level programs the teachers considered successful. Other teachers noted incompatibilities with their personal conceptions of good teaching. This sentiment may be a reflection of the tension between an emerging view of professionalism as collective responsibility for standards of practice versus the view of professionalism as individual autonomy that has previously predominated in teaching.

A paradox is that while most teachers agreed that "the district holds high expectations for schools" and felt that "the district invests in high quality professional development for teachers," many also voiced mistrust of the district's motives and support for school-level reforms. In this sense, distributed leadership—that is, complementary district and teacher roles based on comparative advantage—was slow to take hold. In the second year of the reform, almost three-quarters of the teachers surveyed felt the pressure of mandates and perceived inadequate support. While recognizing that the district "holds high standards for their schools" (71%), fewer than half agreed that the district "helps schools focus on teaching and learning" (45%), "emphasizes academic standards at all levels" (41%), or "has consistent standards across schools" (40%). A very small minority agreed that the district "inspires teachers to perform their best" (12%), and consults with (4%) or learns from (11%) school staff. Although the district's theory of instruction placed professional accountability with teachers, teachers had little sense of district efforts to institutionalize their participation or promote teacher leadership. In these areas, as in others, secondary teachers were least optimistic (see Table 4.6).

One instructional leader explained how the reform collided directly with the strong emphasis on site-based governance that had been negotiated in the previous contract under the prior administration:

The last contract from the union with the district gave the site governance teams the most power they've ever had in years: to look at budgets, to look at master schedules, to look at teacher placement. . . . If the principal said "no" to what the governance team said, it would go through an appeals process at the district level. I mean, they had negotiated the most powerful site governance package that had ever come down the pike. And that was last year [1997–1998]. This year [1998–1999], here comes, "Central Office will tell the sites what to do." And that's not the fault of the teachers or the school. Someone else brought that site governance culture to us. I mean, it was pervasive throughout the United States, and you were told repeatedly, "The sites know best; the sites will make the decisions about budgets, decisions

Table 4.6. Teachers' Views of District Support for Teachers and Schools

Proportion of Teachers Agreeing[1] That:	All Teachers (n = 404)	Elementary School	Middle School	High School
This district creates mandates without providing adequate support	74%	77%	70%	71%
The district holds high expectations for our school	71%	77%	62%	60%
This district helps schools focus on teaching and learning	45%	45%	22%	18%
The district emphasizes academic standards at all levels of the system	41%	50%	25%	25%
This district has consistent standards from school to school	40%	46%	34%	31%
The district is committed to high standards for every student	37%	45%	26%	23%
This district invests in high-quality professional development for teachers	34%	47%	21%	9%
The district ensures that student learning is the "bottom line" in schools	27%	38%	11%	9%
This district helps schools use information about students' achievement relative to standards in order to improve instruction	21%	27%	8%	13%
This district provides support to enable teachers to adjust curriculum and instruction to meet all students' individual needs	13%	18%	7%	5%
I feel that this district inspires the very best in the job performance of its teachers	12%	15%	8%	5%
This district provides all schools the same level and kind of support for reform	11%	10%	14%	13%
District administrators visit and learn from school administrators and staff	11%	15%	6%	5%
The district promotes teacher leadership across district schools	9%	11%	7%	2%
The district office consults with schools on issues that affect schools	4%	4%	4%	3%

[1]Percentage responding 4 or 5 on a 5-point Likert Scale where 5 is "strongly agree" or "a great deal."
Source: CTP Teacher Survey, Spring 2001.

about staffing, decisions about programs; the sites will interview for principals; the sites will interview for teachers." So here comes the new one that says, "We are the Institute for Learning. We will approve or disapprove what comes your way. We have a new process for selecting principals. We may or may not get your input at some stage." There was a little to-do about that.

District–Union Relations

Teachers' views about the process of change reflected the deteriorating relationship between the San Diego Education Association (SDEA) and the district management. Tensions between the district and the union initially surfaced publicly during the protracted conflict over the new peer coach position that Alvarado wanted to create in schools during the 1998–1999 school year. The district leadership and the teachers union disagreed on selection and reporting procedures for these new positions. The teachers union was concerned about having input into the selection of peer coaches and about the possibility that coaches would be evaluating their own colleagues. Meanwhile, the district leaders wanted to select the peer coaches to ensure their quality. This disagreement postponed the implementation of peer coaches until the fall of 1999 and set the stage for later conflict over the "Blueprint."

By March of 2000, when Bersin and Alvarado presented the final draft of the "Blueprint" to the board, large protests by teachers, classroom aides, and some parents greeted them. Among the issues was the large reduction in the numbers of paraprofessionals as part of the plan to redirect resources to teaching and professional development. One of two board members who requested (unsuccessfully) to postpone the decision to adopt the plan commented: "Anything that gets implemented (in the fall) will be hampered from the onset by this climate. . . . There are a lot of unhappy, suspicious and unsatisfied people."[4] The teachers union president, Marc Knapp, asserted, "This plan as presented will not achieve the success we all want for our students because the people that know how to make it go were not asked."[5]

While Alvarado and Bersin regretted the teacher and parent opposition, they asserted that the district needed to do what was best for improving instruction, not what was best for the classroom aides. They confronted critics with SDCS's troubling statistics. Alvarado argued:

When we have 65 percent of our students not meeting grade level standards, over 30 percent of them dropping out, and fully 75 percent of those who graduate and go to community college and the state system not being able to take a college course because they have to take remedial reading and math, we have to change that. The burden of proof is [on] someone who wants to defend the existing system because it's not even close to what an American urban system has to be in order to promote some kind of justice to its students.[6]

The responses of many teachers who felt simultaneously professionally invigorated and stunned can be seen as a result of the district's "act now, explain later" approach that prioritized speed of implementation over up-front buy-in from stakeholders. Reflecting on this approach, one top-ranking district official explained:

[O]ne of the things that is important about having people participate in change is that they give their buy-in right from the start. But on the other hand, trying to get buy-in sometimes sacrifices the reform or the effort that you're trying to do. So, [we've been] challenge[d] to figure out a balance between that—the buy-in, the speed of the change, the importance of the innovation, keeping the innovation itself pure so that it isn't . . . compromised. . . . And I think that we had to make a decision about which was more important and . . . urgent. And the urgency was to do something about student achievement and to get the innovations and interventions in place. And so what was sacrificed might have been a lot of the time it takes for buy-in and a lot of the compromise [that results] from buy-in.

As a consequence of this strategy for change, in the first 3 years of the reform, the teachers union often felt included by the district only after major decisions already had been made. In our interviews and document review, we found a strong similarity in how teachers talked about reform implementation and what the union publications said about the reform; at times the responses seemed almost scripted. One outside observer noted that the dissenting teachers union, which has a myriad of mature communications networks, "is writing the story because the district doesn't have the resources or skills to write it itself."

This fractured relationship ultimately complicated and sometimes thwarted various aspects of the reform, at times impeding the district's attempts to reallocate fiscal and human resources toward its instructional agenda. For instance, throughout the duration of this study, San Diego was unable to fully address the tendency—shared with most other urban districts—for more experienced teachers to flock to the least needy schools. San Diego did not manage to redesign its internal assignment processes or introduce incentives for individuals teaching in hard-to-staff schools. Similarly, the district would have liked to create additional peer coaching roles using state resources associated with the state's Peer Accountability and Review (PAR) program. However, union negotiations around PAR resulted in a more traditional allocation of these funds, most of which went directly to schools to use as they saw fit, within broad guidelines established by SDCS and SDEA.

Furthermore, the acrimonious relationship between the district and union influenced teachers' views about the change *process* as one that was top-down and noninclusive of teachers' views. Our survey results reflect this attitude. However, we also found that most teachers voiced significant support for most of the instructional changes introduced by district officials, as well as for outcomes of the reforms, such as greater principal skills, peer collegiality, and high-quality professional development. Focused central-office attention to the details of instruction—with the subsequent accountability measures in place to remove inadequate performers—created a delicate blend of emotions including excitement, efficacy, fear, pride, and sometimes resentment from those within schools.

The change from a local-control model of school management to a more centralized approach was not an easy one. Overall, our research suggests that during the first 2 to 3 years of San Diego's reform implementation, principals and teachers valued structural changes such as Learning Communities, walk-throughs, the Literacy Block, and professional-development activities. However, the survey data did not portray the kind of strong distributed leadership that is intended to undergird reciprocal accountability. Teachers' negative reaction to the district's centralized reform was based on their view that district leaders dismissed the teachers' professional knowledge. As the reform unfolded, teachers increasingly demanded to see research upon which the strategies were built. They also expressed interest in reading about New York's Community School District No. 2 (upon which many aspects of the San Diego reform was modeled) and learning about its structure and operations. Additionally, they wanted to see research and cases of exemplary practice from *within* SDCS, where policy and professional contexts were immediate.

The district began to make these local exemplars available, selecting teachers to become staff developers and coaches who conducted demonstration lessons, and creating special "lab" classrooms outfitted with multiple video cameras and a two-way mirror where teachers could watch expert teachers conduct their daily teaching; the observers could then evaluate their colleagues' moves and debrief their decisions. As chapters 5 through 8 illustrate, we documented a trend toward greater consistency in teaching practices and greater comfort with the practices being modeled over the 4 years of this study. Moreover, while teachers were initially uncomfortable with aspects of the reforms, we found that as time went on, professional accountability and distributed leadership gradually took root at the school level. At the same time, school norms and capacities mediated district reforms in significant ways. We now turn to the story of how reform played out at the school level in elementary, middle, and high schools.

NOTES

1. Downloaded from pqasb.pqarchiver.com/sandiego/mai on August 1, 2001.

2. This is a significantly larger proportion than principals surveyed in a comparison sample in the San Francisco Bay area. The San Diego survey was administered by CTP to all principals in the district, and had a response rate of 89%. Bay Area principals were surveyed in 1998 as part of an evaluation of the Bay Area School Reform Collaborative (BASRC). Of 221 member principals surveyed, 131 responded, representing 129 schools in 53 Bay Area districts for a response rate of 59%.

3. The comparable proportion in the Bay Area comparison group (see note 2) was even lower, at 50%. See McLaughlin et al., 1999.

4. Maureen Magee, "Sweeping School Reform is Approved; 3-2 Decision Made Despite Thousands of Protesters," *San Diego Union-Tribune*, March 15, 2000, p. A-1.

5. Magee, "Sweeping School Reform is Approved," p. A-1.

6. Magee, "Battle Over the 'Blueprint'; School Overhaul Plan, Up for Vote Today, Splits District," *San Diego Union-Tribune*, March 14, 2000, p. B-1.

CHAPTER 5

Reform at the Elementary Level:
Changing Practice, Changing Culture

Because the initial focus of San Diego's efforts was literacy, the reforms fit most naturally at the elementary level. Not only is teaching reading integral to the role of the elementary teacher, but elementary schools are somewhat more organizationally malleable than secondary schools. Elementary schools are generally smaller, the faculty is not fragmented along disciplinary lines, and it is possible for the principal to have enough content knowledge across multiple subject areas to serve as an instructional leader. Thus, one would expect that for reasons of both fit and emphasis, the district's reform strategy would find the most traction at the elementary level. Indeed, this appeared to be the case.

Using student achievement as a bottom-line indicator, the district sharply improved elementary student performance in the aggregate and reduced achievement gaps among subpopulations of concern. In addition to the fact that test scores for San Diego's elementary students improved more steeply than did the scores in the state as a whole, reading scores for English-language learners on the SAT-9 rose more rapidly than those of their non-ELL peers from 1998 to 2002, as did scores of African American, Latino, and Indo-Chinese students as compared to White and Asian students (Quick et al., 2003).

On average, the 10 lowest-performing schools—the district's "focus schools" that receive additional targeted resources—closed the gap between high- and low-performing students faster than other district schools. The percentage of students scoring at or above the 50th percentile in reading increased 12 points for the focus schools as compared to 8 points for all other elementary schools (San Diego Achievement Forum, 2002). Similarly, the percentage of students in the lowest quartile decreased by 25 points in the focus schools compared to 14 points for all other elementary schools (San Diego Achievement Forum, 2002). Compared to schools statewide that fell in the lowest decile on the Academic Performance Index (API), the focus schools posted significantly larger gains in reading on the SAT-9, while performance on the standards-based portion of the state tests was comparable (Quick et al., 2003). Taken together, these achievement data suggest that at the elementary level in San Diego, the instructional reforms boosted student learning and contributed to more equitable outcomes for historically underserved students. (See Appendix for data.)

This chapter offers a sketch of how the district's reform strategies played out in elementary schools, based on survey and interview data we collected from teachers and principals in a cross section of high-, medium-, and low-performing elementary schools over several years. We found that over time, the district's focus on a well-articulated literacy program yielded greater understanding and consistency in instructional strategies among elementary school teachers. The emphasis on equity and meeting individual student needs translated into teachers' learning how to teach students at their skill and knowledge levels and move them up, rather than offering undifferentiated instruction targeted at the middle. Elementary principals, in particular, took on the challenge of instructional leadership and gained a deeper knowledge of literacy as a result the district's expectations of the central place of instructional knowledge in the principalship. Finally, there emerged a kind of professional accountability among colleagues that was predicated on principal and teacher learning of and expertise in specific instructional strategies. While we saw persistent tensions between organized teachers and the district, we also observed the appearance of a strong ethic that practice should be based on knowledge and skill and that educators owe to students a duty of care, which includes increasing their own capacities.

We discuss these themes within the context of elementary schools, turning first to the instructional focus of the reforms, then to the system of professional learning that supported instruction, and last to the accountability measures that motivated and bolstered change.

LITERACY AT THE CENTER

As we have noted, San Diego reformers placed at the center of their efforts a set of research-based instructional strategies—beginning with literacy—that guided professional development for principals and teachers and that principals and teachers were accountable for understanding and implementing. The process of change was intense and difficult. By 2002, instructional leaders rated just under a third of the elementary schools as high implementers of the "Blueprint" (Quick et al., 2003, p. II-6). Teachers struggled to create common meaning around the literacy strategies while applying them within their particular school and student contexts. Furthermore, because the reform message emphasized bringing up the lowest-performing students, teachers at low- and high-performing schools responded to the reform goals differently. By 2002, however, teachers at the elementary level reported using the instructional strategies more frequently than did middle and high school teachers (Quick et al., 2003), and virtually all schools had incorporated at least some of the strategies.

Implementing a Balanced-Literacy Approach in the Classroom

The focus on balanced literacy was an explicit directive to all schools in the district, a prescription that rankled among some elementary school teachers. Nevertheless, teachers saw tangible signs that the district was serious about supporting instructional change, the first being the materials that arrived in the classrooms. First-grade teachers each received $5,000 for classroom materials; their counterparts in the lowest-performing schools received $8,000. As one teacher recounted, she went from having one basal reader that started at the wrong level, consulting a list of big books that were available at the library, and spending at least $2,500 of her own money each year to having almost more materials than she could use.

Learning the strategies to make use of the materials was the next step. This took time to develop. In the first year of reform, the focus on guided reading helped establish a common language among elementary teachers. This common language facilitated professional discourse—for example, describing what well-executed reading instructional strategies look like and expressing the development of students' reading skills. As one teacher observed during the second year of the reforms:

[O]ne of the positive aspects of having a focus is using the same language to describe what's expected of the students with their goals or standards. "Using the same language" means a lot, I think, across the school and across the district.

A common language also gave teachers and principals a sense that *all* schools were receiving the same message from the district. Although controversy abounded regarding what teachers perceived as a centralized, one-size-fits-all district reform, the advantage lay in opportunities for schools with the most challenging student populations to receive the same types of professional development and opportunities as other schools. According to elementary school principals, this was not the case in the past, and they took it as an indicator of more equitable treatment of schools by the district.

Accountability pressures also increased during this early period, even as teachers had yet to grasp what guided reading looked like in practice. By the second year, the pressure on principals increased the pressure on teachers. As one teacher explained, her principal took on the attitude that "my job isn't to tell you what you're doing well, but what you need to change." In this climate, the new instructional strategies did penetrate classroom practice in elementary schools. One relatively novice teacher observed that, in a variety of ways, his students were demonstrating improved reading comprehension.

The scores are higher on the DRA [Developmental Reading Assessment, a district diagnostic test]. The way the kids are talking, the language they are using, they really are becoming independent learners. . . . I do know this: The quality of talk . . . has changed through this year as compared to last year. We are actually having book talks and we are sitting around the circle and they are holding up their books and they are talking about their predictions and their realizations. These are first graders and they are actually holding these predictions in their heads, and they have these book conversations that they didn't have last year.

Teachers using the literacy strategies thus started seeing changes in their students' performance. The frequency of these accounts increased after a few years, when both teachers and students had become more proficient with the strategies.

Consistency in literacy instruction from classroom to classroom also became more evident over time. By the third year of the reforms, principals observed that teachers had a better understanding of strategies like read-alouds and shared reading. As one principal noted, teachers also had a common understanding of what it meant to have a purpose and focus to a lesson. Another principal thought that the training and focus on literacy were beginning to reduce discrepancies in teaching quality:

> The biggest amount of change is in the way they're teaching reading. They really are teaching immensely different[ly]. . . . They understand the importance of teaching reading strategies. They understand the importance of teaching phonemic awareness. They understand the importance of really having students read. It used to be you'd walk in the classroom and you might sit there all morning and the kids were doing worksheets or they were doing activities but they REALLY weren't reading. . . . Right now, that's a little uneven. But you see that's where when you "go deep," that unevenness begins to go away. When we first started this, it was very, very uneven from teacher to teacher. Now it is not as uneven.

One math-specialist educator, a former teacher who was with the district during the first years of the Bersin/Alvarado tenure and who is now working closely with low-performing schools, observed a significant difference in how teachers approach their literacy instruction after 4 years of targeted effort:

> When you walk into the schools, it's clear that teaching and learning are going on. There's no down time. Students are being held accountable, teachers have a set of behaviors they are going through that matches what shared reading, guided reading looks like.

This and other accounts of classroom practice suggest that the district's relentless push to implement specific literacy strategies contributed to more thorough and consistent literacy expertise across schools and classrooms.

Learning to Teach Students Where They Are

District leaders emphasized that teachers need to meet students at their level of skills and knowledge development. In classrooms with wide-ranging abilities, this means that teachers need to know the reading level of each student and tailor instruction to individuals and small groups in ways that meet each student's needs, rather than teaching the whole group with strategies targeted at the middle. The notion of teaching the student—not the curriculum—requires classroom assessments that can inform teachers about individual student development. It also requires that teachers have a repertoire of strategies to meet a variety of needs in the same classroom.

Over the course of the first years of the reform, principals reported that their staffs were making significant progress towards more systematically evaluating individual students for diagnostic and instructional-planning purposes. As one noted:

> If you were to see our school now as compared with last year, we are much more clear about our purpose and what it is that we need to teach children. We are much more analytical, right down to the child's level . . . where each child should be at a reading level, at what time of year. . . . I have a sheet on every teacher and the children's names are listed there with their DRA—which is Developmental Reading Assessment— level, their guided reading level, and their equivalent as to what grade level that would be.

The extent to which these approaches were becoming routine was suggested by a teacher who was involved in assessing her students and adapting instruction to their needs. She noted, "In literacy, that's just what you do, [you] wouldn't think of doing otherwise."

As a standard for equity, the district broadcast strong messages about reducing the percentage of students in the bottom quartiles (and then later, the bottom quintiles to reflect the state's five-level performance scale). Identifying all of the Q1 and Q2 (first and second quartile) students individually by classroom and school provided teachers and principals the opportunity to confront the circumstances of individual students, to direct and coordinate resources and supports, and to incorporate specific students' learning needs into lesson plans. Teachers were required to write individualized literacy plans that incorporated elements of the district "Blueprint"—intervention, prevention, and acceleration—for each student who was significantly below grade level. The main thrust of the reforms was clearly to aid the lowest-performing students in meeting grade-level content standards, although district leaders argued that all students benefit when the lowest-performing improve. That is, the leaders' goal was to "lift the base of instruction across the whole system so the academic achievement of all students rises" (San Diego School Board, 2000, p. 1).

Not surprisingly, low- and high-performing schools experienced the district's literacy work in different ways. While low-performing schools began to receive resources more commensurate with their students' needs, the pressure to improve also mounted. In relatively high-performing schools, framing equity issues in terms of individual student needs—not only as differences among subpopulations—helped teachers reshape their perspective from "the school as a whole is performing well" to "not every student is meeting grade-level standards but all should be expected to." Relatively high-performing schools increased their energies on those in the bottom quartiles, but also grappled with how to attend to high-achieving students who did not receive the extra resources that were channeled to struggling students. This principal of a relatively high-performing school described her approach this way:

> As I do my daily observations I have a list of the kids in each room that are Q1 and the interactions that they are having with the teachers. I am kind of trying to keep track of that. . . . In a school like mine, the feeling is that you are giving these kids all the extra attention, doing all these kinds of things for Q1 and Q2 and as they are getting better certainly you are trying also to think about the kids who are the high achievers.

Teachers at high-performing schools generally felt less urgency about changing teaching strategies than did their peers in low-performing schools, because more of the students at high-performing schools entered school already reading. Due to their sense of relative accomplishment, teachers tended to be more critical of the district mandates. At one school that had historically performed well on standardized tests, the principal described the reactions of a staff reluctant to implement some aspects of the reform.

> So for some of these components of the literacy program, it has been a little bit difficult for people. [For example], this whole idea of going to a three-hour Literacy Block every day has been a real push. Because we

were not one of the focus schools, we did not have to have our three-hours first thing in the morning. We have had a little bit of leeway and I have tried to give teachers that leeway. . . . At first, it was a bit of a struggle. Teachers kept saying three hours of this?! and we have slowly shown how they can bring other content areas into that three-hour Literacy Block, especially my upper grade teachers. It has taken a lot of work with them.

These teachers, like others, wanted some flexibility that would acknowledge that they could remain faithful to the intent of the reforms while serving their students in ways that reflected their professional understanding of their own students' academic needs. While applauding the focus on having students read, teachers sometimes chafed under the district's uniform approach. Teachers reported that the rapid pace of change and the top-down process did not always give them time "to identify and see the value in this wonderful idea," as one put it.

The district put forth an ambitious vision of literacy instruction and charged principals and teachers with raising the achievement of the students who struggled most. Despite the struggles inherent in an intensive, rapid change process, the reform generated substantial energy through the system and began to build a common knowledge base across teachers and schools. The goal of deepening instructional knowledge throughout the district—across schools and among certificated and administrative staff—was at the center of extensive new professional-learning structures, which we discuss below.

Developing a System of Learning

The initial objectives of the elaborate professional-learning system in San Diego were to implement the district-defined balanced-literacy strategies (and later mathematics and other subjects) and raise the achievement of the lowest-performing students. The structures were intended to embed adult learning within the school and to connect it to teachers' daily practice. This approach required both a large cultural change in school organizations and new structural supports.

The cultural change began with redefining the district system as one of learners at all levels—instructional leaders, principals, teachers, and staff developers—all of whom were responsible for their own learning and that of their peers, as well as of those who reported to them in the district hierarchy. District leaders developed professional-learning strategies and structures for all school levels—including workshops and institutes, networks, and coaching—but these were most highly developed at the elementary level. Alvarado's experiences in Community District No. 2 in New York City, an elementary school district, gave him deep knowledge of instructional change at this level. Furthermore, elementary teachers and principals were most prone to seeing literacy as part of their mission. Thus, not surprisingly, district leaders' efforts to build principal and teacher expertise found the most traction at the elementary level, while high school principals' and teachers' needs were relatively unmet until later (see chapter 8).

The district's vision of professional learning entailed individual as well as organizational change. Teachers and principals were guided, encouraged, and, in some cases, prodded to take the stance of a learner, to be comfortable with uncertainty and to see improvement as a continuous and neverending quest. In the words of one principal, "[We became] much more willing to live in question instead of having to have the answer right now." The message was to risk change, at least within the district's definition of balanced literacy. Experimentation and inquiry were tools to pursue student learning toward clearly articulated goals for literacy (and later, mathematics and science) learning. Both principals and teachers participated in significantly different and more intense learning activities in the service of improving instruction and meeting student needs.

Principal Learning

Under the district's theory of change, the expectation that principals were to be instructional leaders at their sites required that they learn in depth how to teach literacy so that they could facilitate teachers' learning. Indeed, many elementary school principals reported that they gained more knowledge about literacy instruction than they had when they were teachers. As one remarked:

I think the district has done an excellent job in teaching us about curriculum and instruction. They are really teaching us how to teach reading. I know more about that than I have EVER known. And to imagine 33, 34 years of being in this business [and] just NOW I'm really understanding reading? I think the district's done a good job of that.

Early in the reforms, one principal explained her own uncertain knowledge about literacy instruction and how her understanding was developing as she lead her staff.

[N]ow we're really looking at each of those elements [of balanced literacy]. We're looking at them, we're trying them in our classrooms. We're doing in-service with our staffs and we're going back and looking for evidence coming back. And I think we're fine-tuning it. I really think that's what's valuable about this whole thing. If you'd asked me a year ago about read-alouds and shared reading, I would have had an answer for you. But . . . shared reading is not what I really thought shared reading [was]. . . . And we're all understanding a little bit more about what that is and how that is a good approach.

Teachers often remarked upon the change in principals as principals were expected to model the stance of a learner. As one observed:

I think [the principal] has grown as an administrator. I see her as being a learner now, too, with us and before I always thought of her as up here, as you are my boss kind of thing. . . . I really feel at a level like we are learning together. . . . So I have seen her change in her expectations, which have become higher—which is good because it makes my expectations for myself become higher as well as for my kids.

Developing a community of learners among principals such that they were supported in building a community of learners within their schools was another important element of the principals' professional learning. Networks of principals in the same cluster of schools met regularly to work on instructional issues, as did couplings that emerged from these meetings. Principals connected in ways that meaningfully broke the isolation so typical of the principalship in many districts. For example, a principal observed that, over the course of 2 years:

We've gone to each other's campuses; we've had wonderful discussions; we've read books together. We've watched each other's staff development tapes and talked about what we could do better, what kinds of things do we think would help the staff more.

Principals paired up and were expected by their instructional leaders to serve as each other's mirrors and sounding boards. One principal gave this example of her work with her partner:

[I might say,] "When I went into the classrooms today, I looked at questioning [a reading comprehension strategy] and, you know, look at this page." And so we go back and we would read and we would look at this or we'd look at our [video]tapes and go, "Oh, see, this is the way I should have said it. Why didn't I say it like this?" "Oh, I thought that's what I said, but that isn't even what I said to the staff." So it's more really analyzing how effective we are in the words we use. How effective we are in our thinking and in our statements. I think for me that's been the biggest change. And it's really a focus on not behavior and discipline and those kinds of things, but really instruction. That's the biggest change I've seen. It's been wonderful. I've really enjoyed that.

While principals took on instructional leadership, the demands of this role and the pace of the reforms taxed their ability to deal with school operations. Despite efforts to centralize operational support, principals continued to feel torn between spending time in the classroom with their teachers and wrestling with paperwork, facilities, and myriad other administrative duties. As one remarked:

I think that most of use would agree that this is far more exciting than our previous role as plant manager. Because, as our colleagues are saying here, there's an instruction part. I'm much closer with my teachers than I ever have been in 13 years. On the other hand, there's something very public about what's going on. We have not yet been prepared for the fact that now the public has been sent a bill of goods, saying that we are the plant managers. . . . It's this double-edged sword. It's exciting; these meetings prepare us, but we also have to run our schools. . . . [T]here is such a dilemma and the anxiety of managing and balancing time.

Principals we interviewed often expressed a need to have more dialogue with their peers about operational issues and did not really accept the idea that operational concerns could be shunted to the central office. Principals also wanted time to work with their peers on curriculum issues:

> [The] biggest barrier for me is the fact that I don't get to dialogue with my peers about operational issues. Again, if you want me to do Open Court, I need a forum to talk to other principals about how they're implementing Open Court and the problems they have. . . . When you're in a rapid fire—and Tony Alvarado says it, you know it's like, "hey, we're inventing this steam horse as we go along"—there needs to be a structure for dialogue about implementation and operational things, and I think it's a barrier that there isn't that dialogue.

Note that by "operational" this principal means implementation of a curriculum program; this reference is in itself a testament to how deeply the focus on instruction had begun to penetrate principals' view of their work.

The Role of the Peer Coach/Staff Developer

San Diego used the peer coach/staff developer role as a means to insert professional learning into the workplace and school day. While the district continued to use workshops as a professional-development format, often the workshops were site based, offered by the peer coach or the principal, and followed up by coaching on and assessment of the use of the new strategies. Peer coaching was an attempt to provide tailored support to individuals and to bring coherence to a range of staff-development formats.

While peer coaching became widely available throughout the district, in the early years the effectiveness of the coaches varied. In 2002, almost three-quarters of elementary teachers (73%) reported working individually with a peer coach/staff developer and 63% reported being coached in their classrooms. However, smaller numbers (44% and 42%, respectively) rated those experiences "very or moderately useful" (Quick et al., 2003, p. II-18 and p. II-20).

As they forged their new roles, peer coaches tended to approach receptive teachers first (Hightower, 2002). Where a positive relationship was developed, teachers valued the insights of their coaches. Said one relatively novice teacher:

That whole thing of the peer coaching, a lot of people felt threatened by that and at first I did too, but it was an awesome experience because it was never like "why did you do it that way," it was more like "how did you think it went?" From that experience I learned to reflect on my practice. . . . As long as you have someone like [our coach] who is really supportive, nurturing and allowed you to make up your mind and think about your practice, I felt really supported.

Several factors emerged as consequential to a coach's ability to create change among the school staff. The teaching experience of the coaches relative to that of the teachers sometimes influenced whether the coaches were seen as legitimate experts. Some veteran teachers thought that the district's recruitment of relatively new teachers (who were typically in their fourth or fifth year of teaching) for coaching positions indicated a lack of respect for the veterans' extensive experience and knowledge. Very experienced teachers at one school, for example, were offended by the idea that they needed a staff developer, that the staff developer had less experience than most of the faculty, and that the school had no choice in how it would spend the funds that paid her salary. In addition, school norms of collaboration (or conversely, of privacy) conditioned whether teachers felt threatened by the presence of colleagues in their classrooms.

Even at schools with large proportions of new teachers, staff developers struggled to establish productive relationships as they straddled the line between peer and expert. The uncharted territory of peer coach became more complex when teachers suspected that their "peer" might be informally evaluating them or reporting back to the principal. In more punitive environments, the coach was sometimes perceived as the principal's "enforcement arm," and teachers were wary of revealing too much.

A final challenge for the coaching process was the number of coaches available. Eventually, the peer coaches took on the role of support provider for beginning teachers, and were funded by the state Beginning Teacher Support and Assessment (BTSA) program. This situation had the advantage of basing the *content* of new-teacher support on the tenets of balanced literacy while differentiating approaches to match the needs of novices. However, for schools with high proportions of new teachers, the staff-developer position did not suffice to meet the needs of both the new teachers and the rest of the faculty. As one principal noted:

> We have over 65 percent of our teachers who have 3 years or less. And that's been tough because what they've done is taken the BTSA money and they put it into a second peer coach. Well at a school like this, it's a pretty unrealistic formula to expect two peer coaches to deal with 68 percent of the staff.

Overall, in cases where the peer coach/staff developer was a respected member of the school faculty, the position represented a valuable resource for teachers. But the ability of individual coaches to engage teachers meaningfully and catalyze change in the classroom varied with time and availability of coaches, coach expertise, legitimacy, level of need at the school, and school norms of privacy or collaboration.

Extensive Learning Opportunities for Teachers

District-led learning opportunities for teachers proliferated under the reform initiative, and teachers reported that they participated in a range of traditional and nontraditional professional-development activities. Roughly two-thirds of elementary teachers reported receiving more than 32 hours of professional development in literacy in the 2001–2002 academic year, more than four times the percentage of elementary teachers nationally (16%) who reported more than 32 hours of professional development in the subject of their main teaching assignment (Quick et al., 2003, p. II-13).

In addition to the on-site staff development resulting from changes in the role of the principal and the addition of peer coaches, almost all teachers reported collaborating regularly with their colleagues, as well as attending summer/intersession institutes and workshops after school and on Saturdays (Quick et al., 2003, p. II-18). As we reported in chapter 4, most elementary teachers found these sessions helpful, and the training evolved in response to teacher feedback. As one principal noted in the third year of the reform, "Teachers continue to be trained by the Institute for Learning; they continue to come back and love it and feel it's worthwhile."

Summer institutes were judged most worthwhile when they covered topics in depth over the period of a week or more. More problematic were the occasions that modeled more traditional "in-servicing" with 1-day workshops, where teachers were expected to master a set of new ideas and then come back and train other teachers. These contrasting assessments of the different kinds of training by principals illustrate the distinctions:

> There seems to be a lot of course offerings, much more. . . . Oh, the Summer Institute classes were. . . . The teachers LOVED them. I think the Summer Institute for Learning helped a lot. Those teachers who attended the training this summer, they came back and they really are much more knowledgeable than we are because they've had a whole week, sometimes, of shared reading or guided reading. . . . Thinking about them having to be the experts in your school and using them, that's making them feel empowered also.
>
> The people who did go over the summer were pretty much expected to come back and train everyone else. . . . And what the teachers get is watered down because it's new to the ones who went to the training. It was a one-day, one-shot training, and they're expected to come back and be an expert of sorts.

The most effective professional development occurred when principals were able to construct an ongoing strand of coherent learning opportunities throughout the year and draw upon a cadre of well-trained teachers to model and support staff learning about specific strategies over a sustained period of time. As one principal described:

> I had some teachers that took part in summer school and then we did the staff development each day and they were given lots of material. The district did a nice job of providing lots of literacy materials last summer and so that was another way they grew professionally. This year . . . we started out with running records and that was one of the things that we learned last summer. We had the Reading Recovery teachers that taught our block about running records and then I used the teachers that worked that summer to be models for us when we did an in-service on running records with the other teachers. We all had a chance to do running records. The expectation was that they would do running records on two of their students from last summer throughout the summer and document

that, and then I had a chance to go into the summer classes . . . and actually do some running records also, which gave me a chance to practice
that, and then when we in-serviced the rest of the staff, I try to use those
teachers. We did a year [of staff development] on running records. When
we talk about guided reading I have a list from the institute [of teachers
who] took part in the guided reading classes this summer, and I call on
them to share some things and do some presentations. So that helped. It
helps the credibility of teachers when they know these are regular classroom teachers that are doing it in their room, and then I have them present how they are using that in their room. So I think that has helped all
of our learning by using other teachers that have had that training.

In addition to formal professional-development sessions, learning
opportunities were built into the school day. Teachers' lounges became
Teacher Learning Centers replete with professional reading libraries
and meeting space for professional conversation. The introduction of
math specialists in the 10 lowest-performing schools relieved upper elementary teachers to engage in literacy professional development during math instructional time. Many teachers voiced appreciation of the
professional development, and new teachers were especially vocal
about how much they had learned:

I think being a newer teacher is an advantage because I don't have a
repertoire that I am leaning on from 20 years ago, so this new stuff is like
you tell me what to do [in literacy] and I do it and it works. I have seen
great results in my classroom. The training is great. At our school, we are
fortunate that they have been giving us a lot of books. We still need a lot
more books, and I think in order for this new literacy thing to take place
and really become alive in the classroom we need more books for our
classrooms. . . . [T]he kids are running out of books because they are
reading so much.

Another major shift was the effort to ground professional learning in
observations and analyses of classroom practice. As we have noted, the
professional-learning structure in San Diego included a greater instructional role for principals, who would be supported by their own Learning Communities, and peer coaches/staff developers who carried professional development into the daily work of teachers. Consistent and
frequent walk-throughs by district administrators and principals and

coaching inside the classroom became the foundation for professional discourse throughout the district. Conversations between ILs and principals, between principals and teachers, and between peer coaches and teachers revolved around the classroom observations.

Cultural changes in the closed-door ethic of schools were needed to stimulate the practice of peer observations. In some schools that had a history of collaboration around instruction, this was not difficult to accomplish. In others, it took time and creativity to help teachers feel comfortable in looking at one another's classrooms. One successful strategy was to observe practice in other schools. Principals and teachers reported more cross-school visitations and observations as teaching practice became more public. For example, one principal had all of her teachers visit schools with the highest test score gains in the district. In this case, teachers were less intimidated by visiting peers in other schools than by watching colleagues teach in their own schools, so authentic collaborative work within their own schools was more difficult to accomplish. As one principal explained:

> The one thing I am NOT as successful at yet is having them leave their classrooms and do observations with their peer teachers on staff. . . . And I've been more successful when I've been able to provide subs or release time having to go to a different school and observe a different teacher. They're willing to do that. The comfort level is still not here with their peers coming in observing or them observing their peers. Even though there are some great things going on, they've got wonderful teachers, it's still that feeling that I'm a teacher, and I really don't know more than you, and I don't really want you coming in observing me if I'm going to be your buddy for the rest of the year.

Over time, peer observation within many schools became a new norm, usually after staff had become more comfortable with discussing one another's practice in team meetings and professional-development settings. Videotapes of practice were increasingly used, along with actual classroom visits, to provide a basis for professional conversations. Analyzing actual, observed instances of teaching practice was the mechanism by which adults built common understandings about the quality of instruction and created tangible ways of altering approaches to better meet student needs. This constant dialogue thus helped deepen the instructional knowledge of all involved.

The fact that discourse and observations of the actual classroom practice formed the crux of professional learning in San Diego was a radical departure from professional-development activities pursued in most districts. This approach placed learning about instruction within the regular, constitutive work of teachers, rather than treating professional development as an adjunct activity that occurred outside of the classroom and school. Pressures to change immediately reinforced these learning opportunities; the underlying message to teachers was learn, but learn quickly, so that students will benefit as soon as possible.

BUILDING PROFESSIONAL ACCOUNTABILITY

Traditional norms of privacy in school organizations present a formidable challenge to incorporating learning within teachers' work. As elementary teachers pursued some of the district-directed learning opportunities and principals worked to create learning communities within their schools, greater transparency in individual teachers' work and more joint work formed a critical foundation for professional accountability. In other words, breaking down the norms of privacy to promote shared understandings of practice—values, goals, and expectations for the quality of instruction and for student performance—became part of the reform process. Professional accountability in the district rested upon these shared understandings.

Strategies for Building Professional Accountability

Several elements of the reform helped promote professional accountability. The shared vocabulary of literacy built through professional development formed the common content that described what all teachers and principals were expected to learn and was the language that permitted professional discourse. Coaching and walk-throughs provided windows into instructional practices, creating expectations that what teachers and principals learned about balanced literacy should be visible and tangible in the classroom.

Walk-throughs in San Diego were both a vehicle for the principals' learning and a check on the kinds of teaching that were occurring in the schools. With this dual purpose, walk-throughs could be intimidating to teachers, especially in schools not accustomed to district administrators' (or anyone's) visits. One principal tried to defuse the potential tension by reinforcing that the walk-throughs are to evaluate the principal, not the teachers. Another principal was able to mediate the walk-throughs by more explicitly emphasizing the learning aspects of the activity and presenting the instructional leader as a resource for the school.

> [Our Instructional Leader and I] meet for about the first 45 minutes or so just going over plans, looking at our teacher evaluations, kind of how we're keeping track of teachers we're evaluating and I show her the documentation I have on those and the feedback I give to teachers. . . . She and I will actually do classroom visits. So I develop a schedule letting teachers know that. And they're about only ten minutes each. We get into the classroom, and we are looking for shared reading when we come. And I always give them a list of what kinds of things we're looking for: shared reading, stating a purpose, and making connections. . . . The nice thing is I always try to build in time for [the IL] to meet with the teachers. So either before school begins or during recess time, she's in the lounge, available to meet with them after . . . so they have a chance to at least . . . so they know her and have a chance to ask questions if they need to.

As the pressure to improve student performance increased over the first couple of years of the reform, however, some teachers detected a shift in the nature of the feedback they received. Initially, they received immediate feedback based on what the principals were learning in their own Learning Communities. A former teacher recounted that as the reforms intensified, her principal and IL appeared to discuss individual teachers after a walk-through and began to provide more prescriptive feedback. In other words, the feedback no longer resembled reflective comments indicative of what principals were learning. Rather, the feedback to teachers became more directive and carried with it an evaluative element. This shift created anxiety, as did some of the other means for opening up and sharing practice, even though there was growing agreement about the success of the reforms. As one teacher noted:

> You know everyone I talk to says that they love what is being done, and they see results; they don't like the way it was pushed on them. That is the only thing. Everyone does recognize that this change is bringing about results; it is just the way . . . and the whole thing with the videotaping. It is like some people have this paranoia, like it is Big Brother you know.

Many people echoed this refrain—that the reform was the "right thing to do" and the practices were successful, but the implementation process created deep-seated anxiety for a number of teachers and principals. Over the 4 years of the study, we saw the practices become more widespread and familiar, and we heard teachers report that they were more comfortable and confident in their abilities to teach all children to read. However, continuing state and local accountability pressures, augmented by federal pressures created by the "adequate yearly progress" standards of No Child Left Behind, meant that the anxiety did not evaporate. In contrast to some districts, though, practitioners in San Diego had acquired a range of productive classroom strategies to use in confronting these pressures.

Building New Norms of Practice

Although the degree to which schools were able to achieve cultural change varied, most schools developed noticeably stronger norms around making instruction a joint enterprise and began to build a sense of professional accountability. To be sure, traditional test-based accountability pressed on the schools, as the district sent clear messages about improving student achievement as measured primarily by state tests. However, professional accountability—that is, accountability for taking the stance of a learner, for the quality of instruction, for collaboration, and for a tangible emphasis on student equity—increased alongside the demands for achievement.

Building professional accountability that revolved around deep instructional knowledge among teachers and principals meant that teachers had to become comfortable discussing how they made instructional decisions, including how they chose materials, whether and how they grouped students and differentiated instruction, and how they ascertained students' instructional needs. They also had to become comfortable and able to defend these decisions in light of professional knowledge for practice. One principal described the evolution through to the third year of reform in this way:

> Before teachers always had teachers' guides to go through, and you started on page one of a book and you went though until the next story

and all that. But having them think about the needs of their kids and getting to know their kids has been a real challenge for us. . . . We are moving along with the effort and the idea is just to keep talking and letting
them know that they are doing some really good things for kids but
maybe trying something a little differently, assessing kids and then using
that assessment to place and find materials that match that, not just assessing for the standardized testing or something . . . I am seeing them
talk about strategies, comprehension strategies, finding materials that
would teach that strategy rather than trying to see "what do I have and
what can I find in this lesson to teach?" At this time last year they would
have picked a book and said, "Well, let's see, this book teaches comprehension so everybody will get that." They are beginning to talk about,
"Well, what can I find? This kid needs comprehension. . . . What kind of
material can I find for that?"

Principals clearly began to feel accountable for the kinds of instruction
taking place in their schools and for facilitating and monitoring their
teachers' learning the strategies that were the focus of professional development. One principal described her role in implementing read-alouds:

Teachers were asked to begin implementing read-alouds, just reading
aloud with their students. So we had staff development [about the fact
that] they were going to introduce read-alouds. I did my observations
that first part of the year, and I was to observe read-alouds, and then give
them the feedback.

This example of supervisory follow-up to professional learning is de-
ceptively simple, for it illuminates some profound connections not often
present in urban schools. First, the principal was focused on and knowledgeable about a specific component of balanced literacy as the district
defined it. Second, professional development for teachers around read-
alouds had clear follow-up: the principal was to observe teachers' use of
read-alouds in class and give them feedback. Third, the principal—the
teachers' direct supervisor—was responsible for providing feedback
based on systematic, close, and immediate observation of actual teaching, not conversations about the practice or ad hoc, unfocused visits to a
few teachers late in the school year. Fourth, the observation, an integral
part of professional development, was simultaneously the accountability

mechanism: teachers were accountable for implementing read-alouds and for becoming skillful at conducting read-alouds. In elementary schools, where literacy is the premier instructional focus, San Diego reforms helped make deep subject matter and pedagogical content knowledge the object of principals' and teachers' learning and bolstered it with professional accountability that engaged principals in classroom instruction.

Principals began to internalize the activities and responsibilities that district reformers had in mind when they said principals were to be instructional leaders, but, with the reform, principals also felt the increased demands on their time, attention, and energy:

> I think I am being more and more clear about the fact that I'm going to be in those classrooms, observing shared reading, to take the lead as far as staff development for that. . . . In years past, if there were things we wanted our staff to be in-serviced on, we were to pick up the phone and call someone from staff development to come out. . . . [N]ow, WE'RE to be the ones to be giving the in-service. I'm expected to attend lots of different in-service, and then share that with my staff. . . . The expectations are growing, and it's hard trying to be everything to everybody. And that's the hard part of the job. But the classroom visits are really a good part of the job.

It is also important to note here that while principals who remained in the job were highly accountable for learning about teaching literacy, a significant number of principals either chose to leave or were moved out of their posts because district administrators did not consider them successful in learning and leading.

Developing Accountability for Student Equity

Since raising the achievement of the lowest-performing students was an explicit goal of the district, accountability measures also emphasized equitable student-learning opportunities. Principals and teachers reported a greater focus on individual student needs, especially those of struggling students, as an example of how accountability among teachers increased under the district's reforms. For example, this teacher described how *all* teachers were expected to attend to the low-performing students in their classes:

I've seen an accountability level rise among the general teaching staff. Some teachers were always extremely accountable, others less so, of course. People are different. But I've seen the accountability rise so much among teachers; they're concerned about every student because there's so much more going on within this new reading system where they're forced to take a look at each student, whether it be through giving the diagnostic reading assessment or what is going on in the portfolios and such. However, this flashes back to when a teacher notices a student isn't doing well; what do they do with him? The support systems aren't built in there yet.

This teacher also raises the issue of the responsibility of the district to provide supports that enable teachers to accomplish what the district holds them accountable for. While the district dramatically increased professional-development activity, many teachers felt that the pressure to improve student performance—especially for those at the bottom—outstripped the organizational supports they received.

A data-driven approach went hand in hand with accountability for student equity, both within individual schools and district-wide. In particular, diagnostic assessments mandated by the district and supported through training were meant to be key ingredients for teachers' instructional planning, as this principal describes:

> Being a data-driven school means that you take many interim assessments. Teachers look at book levels of kids. We don't want any surprises. We're not waiting for the SAT-9 to come out and tell us what to do. . . . [I tell them,] "You only have 20 kids and you get a pretty good salary. I expect you to know every one of those kids by name, their levels and what next you're going to do to test them with . . . [and] the feedback to get from them to do whatever it is."

Administrators clearly expected teachers to use data on an individual-student basis, in addition to organizational analyses of the percentage of students in the lowest quartiles.

The implications of the emphasis on equitable student learning extended to school operations. For example, in at least one case, the school had to transition from a year-round multitrack schedule to a single track because it could not implement the "Blueprint." During intercession for any given track, the school did not have enough space to provide accelerated learning programs for students below grade level, a cornerstone requirement of the "Blueprint." As this principal described the district:

> The instruction side of the house is calling some of the shots for the financial and operation side of the house. . . . And, boy, is [this school] ever . . . [a] quintessential example of the instruction side of the house making some decisions that formerly I would have had a door shut in my face. "Too bad if you don't have enough classes—put them in the cafeteria."

Another principal echoed the importance of this change:

> I feel I have access to people [at the central office] who are now very service-oriented. That is one thing that Alan Bersin has done; [he] has made the Ed. Center realize that they are in support of teaching and learning. And, boy, do we ever get that feeling now when we call that Ed. Center.

The central-office reorganization, which placed instructional departments in charge, produced different results for schools.

Within the context of state and federal test-based accountability policies, the district moved from emphasizing remediation for students in the lowest two quartiles to those in the lowest two quintiles, a reflection of the California five-level performance scale. Subsequently, as a result of the proficiency standards required by the federal No Child Left Behind legislation, the focus shifted further to include greater attention to students performing at somewhat higher levels. For example, teachers in the 10 lowest-performing schools ("focus schools") were asked to identify five students who were scoring just below "proficient" on the rubric and to concentrate on moving them up to the proficient level. Presumably, those five students served as a bellwether for other students with similar skills, so strategies that assisted the five students in reaching proficiency might also result in others' reaching proficiency. This directive represented a change from focusing primarily on the lowest-performing students to a focus on individualizing instruction throughout the performance range.

Paradoxes of Professional Accountability in a Top-Down Reform

San Diego's approach to creating professional accountability was grounded in instructional strategies that demand sophisticated understanding of subject matter, pedagogy, and students. Even though the district mandated that the strategies be used, they were not scripted in their nature. Instead, the instructional approach rested on the teacher's knowledge and skills, including abilities to assess students' reading levels and the sources of reading errors, to find books at appropriate levels for individual students, to manage a classroom with multiple groups, to conference with individual students during the school day, and to teach reading comprehension strategies. Developing each teacher's expertise took investment and time. The district faced the dilemma of allowing time for discussions about literacy to foster common understanding and knowledgeable teacher decision making while pursuing structural methods of motivating immediate change from the top down. Giving priority to the urgency of supporting today's students, structures such as walk-throughs and peer coaches, and reading protocols enforced by principals and staff developers sometimes felt like top-down pressure to teachers. As one teacher put it:

> We don't have a problem with the strategies you're teaching to us; it's the immediacy and punitive nature [of the reforms]. Teachers are not allowed to be in an approximation zone. They need to show results immediately and are not allowed time to learn.

In this context of rapid-fire change, professional accountability based on norms of developing expertise and shared knowledge was heavily bolstered by more traditional bureaucratic accountability based on expectations that directives from superordinates would be followed. The district's reforms, while heavy handed by some accounts, also offered early evidence of the success of school-level change, which provided leverage for motivating teacher change, as this principal described after a year of the reforms:

> It's the framework, and it doesn't tell me every little piece of how to organize a school, because just like you have to be intentional to your school, you have to be intentional to who the kids are. But at least I come

with a framework and a district behind me. One of the questions that someone asked me on the side, one of the teachers [asked], "You really do this stuff?" "I really do this stuff, and so will you." [The teacher continued,] "I mean, Do you really do all that stuff? Are we going to have to do all that stuff?" [My reply was,] "Yes, you are."

By the nature of the task they faced, bureaucratic forms of accountability—that is, a top-down insistence on implementing district directives—were much more dominant in low-performing schools. Resources were funneled into these schools, as were expectations for sharp growth. While the growth occurred, the hard work, spotlight, and pressure contributed to teacher turnover, which continued to be high at the focus schools, particularly during the last year (2002–2003), when the district offered early-retirement packages. For example, at one school, 39 out of 52 teachers were new in 2002. At another, three out of four math specialists were new to the position. And the district continued to move principals in and out of the focus schools—8 out of 10 were new to the schools in 2002—in search of powerful instructional leadership.

For all of the difficulties, during the years we followed the reforms in San Diego, the rigor, hard work, and pressure yielded some very promising bottom-line results, as this principal described after 1 year:

You know, I want to say first and foremost, my overriding thought about the new leadership is that I've never been more challenged or more enthusiastic in 30 years. I'm seeing more work out of kids, better production of teachers, more commitment, whether it's out of fear or whatever. Whoever knows what it is. I don't care to analyze it. All I know is that this regime has been the best that I've been through in 5 years.

CHAPTER 6

Reform at the Middle School Level:
From the Inside Out

While San Diego's reform strategies were tightly focused on the work of elementary schools, middle schools posed additional challenges, given their departmentalization, generally larger size, and broader mission, including the pressures of preparing students for high school. In order to examine the change process "from the inside out," we conducted in-depth case studies over 3 years in three middle schools that were chosen to reflect similarly diverse student populations but very different organizational structures and cultures. Steward Junior High School, Robinson Middle School, and Laurel Ridge Middle School all serve student populations predominantly comprised of students of color with large numbers of English-language learners and students eligible for the free and reduced-price lunch programs.[1] (Table 6.1 profiles these schools, their reform challenges, and their student performance outcomes.) Before the reform, the schools operated with very different philosophies and in very different ways.

Steward typified many urban junior high schools: At the start of our study, it maintained a traditional six-period schedule; its curriculum was largely rote oriented; student achievement was low; and few opportunities existed for student personalization. Steward teachers rarely collaborated; a large number were uncredentialed and underprepared; and senior staff at this school historically had few learning opportunities through which to deepen their practice.

In contrast to Steward, Robinson Middle School was structurally "reformed," with houses that enabled teams of teachers to work with

Table 6.1. Summary of School Contexts and Changes: Steward, Laurel Ridge, Robinson

	Steward Pre-reform	*Steward amidst Reform*	*Laurel Ridge Pre-reform*	*Laurel Ridge amidst Reform*	*Robinson Pre-reform*	*Robinson amidst Reform*
Working Description, Metaphor	Neglected with respect to leadership and teacher quality. A traditional junior high school: highly tracked; teachers isolated; rote-oriented curriculum.	Feeling strong force of the district "boom," especially regarding expectations for classroom teaching practice.	Professionally active. Some teacher teams and much curriculum innovation. Takes advantage of grants, and sees itself as "out ahead of the district."	Mature professional culture strategically adopting the best of the district reforms. Teachers are most positive regarding the district.	Semiautonomous "schools within a school." Progressive ideology. Some teams very strong; some much weaker. Very uneven practice.	Restructured school feeling the full force of the district "boom." Practice more consistent. but teaming lost. Case of district values trumping school values.
Teacher-Quality Factors— Improvements in all three schools	In 1998, 96% credentialed, 22% emergency credentialed.* Many low-quality teachers, and little discussion of teaching.	In 2000, 100% credentialed, 2% emergency credentialed. Several teachers evaluated out, including probationary and tenured.	In 1998, 98% credentialed, 11% emergency credentialed. Stable staff; many student teachers. Strong support for beginning teachers.	In 2000, 100% credentialed, 0% emergency credentialed. Stable staff; many student teachers. Strong support for beginning teachers, plus peer coaching.	In 1998, 87% credentialed, 24% emergency credentialed. High turnover. Experienced teachers teamed together; newer teachers left together.	In 2000, 100% credentialed, 3% emergency credentialed. Still high turnover. Fewer preps for beginning teachers and more even access to expertise.

*Emergency credentialed teachers may be either uncredentialed or credentialed but assigned to teach outside the field of the credential.

Teaching Quality—Changes in all three schools	Mostly isolated practice. Mostly teacher led, with some pockets of innovative practice. Overall, low expectations for student achievement and poor outcomes.	More public practice. More cross observations, coaching, and improved pockets of teaching. More student independent worktime and one-on-one time with language arts teachers, especially in two-hour block classes. Teachers report having higher expectations for student achievement.	Some teams of teachers share students; much shared professional development, but most classroom practice is teacher centered. Relatively high expectations and coherent curriculum.	Peer coaching and peer observation increased. Teacher-led professional development is more common, and teachers are looking more at student data. More cross observations, coaching, and improved pockets of teaching. More student independent worktime and one-on-one time with language arts teachers, especially in two-hour block classes. Teachers focused on studying and improving student engagement.	Varies substantially by "house," with some houses providing more coherent curriculum than others. Houses vary with respect to taking advantage of common prep times and providing excellent teaching. Some teachers are professionally active, but others do little.	More evenly distributed across the school. More coaching and work with consultants, and more observation of other teachers at other schools and within school. Teachers are looking more at student data. Loss of personalization undermines close student relationships and quality of some teaching, but reforms may improve teaching for others.

(continued)

Table 6.1. Summary of School Contexts and Changes: Steward, Laurel Ridge, Robinson (continued)

	Steward Pre-reform	Steward amidst Reform	Laurel Ridge Pre-reform	Laurel Ridge amidst Reform	Robinson Pre-reform	Robinson amidst Reform
Stratification	Highly tracked with GATE, ELL, and bilingual classes.	More stratification, including sixth grade, which is organized by GATE, bilingual, and Q1/Q2 learning needs.	Some GATE tracking, efforts to mainstream ELL students; two heterogeneous teams and advisory classes.	More stratification with Literacy Block classes (Q1/Q2) with "echoes" throughout other classes.	Some ELL tracking (especially with beginning students), but generally heterogeneous "houses."	More stratification with Literacy Block classes (Q1/Q2) with "echoes" throughout other classes. More GATE stratification. Advisory classes no longer always heterogeneous.
Personalization	Little personalization—traditional schedule with six periods, little teaming. Some special education students have very high personalization, and seminar students have smaller class size in	More personalization with sixth grade. Block classes allow more personalization for low performers. Special education unchanged.	Medium—some teaming and an advisory period. Some special education students have very high personalization, and seminar students have access to smaller classes in English/SS. Spent funds to	Medium—teaming and advisory remain, block and seminar classes allow more personalization for low performers. Special education unchanged. Loss of discretionary	Very high—students have same teachers all year, and in some cases for 3 years. Advisory period. Some special education students have very high personalization.	Medium-low—still have advisory, but no more teams. Block classes allow more personalization for low performers. Reduced personalization impacts student-teacher relationships

	English/social studies.		lower class sizes across subject areas.	money that had kept class size down across the board.		and teacher collaboration and learning.
Teacher-Teacher Time	No common preps (except for three teachers). PD time after school and on AB 777 days.	Common preps for sixth-grade teachers; teachers in same grade more proximate in location. Attempted grade-level interdisciplinary teams.	Only teams have common preps.	Literacy Block teachers have common prep and additional PD hour each day. Teams continue with common preps.	Teacher teams have one hour common prep per day and built-in PD each week (two and one half hours).	No common preps for teachers, still have built-in PD each week (two and one half hours).
Achievement	Well below state averages. API = 2nd decile. 86% of students tested.	Below average but improving. II/USP planning in 2000–2001. Improved nearly 80 points by 2003. API increase of nearly 70 points by 2003. 97% of students tested. (New sixth grade added.)	At about the state average. API = 5th decile. 93% of students tested.	At the state average. Large improvements in 1999–2000 and 2000–2001, but below targets in 2001 for one subgroup. II/USP planning in 2001–2002. API increased by nearly 50 points by 2003. 99% of students tested.	Well below state average. API = 2nd decile. 90% of students tested.	Below average but improving. II/USP planning in 1999–2000. Meets targets and collects rewards in 2000–2001 and 2001–2002. API increase of more than 100 points by 2003. 100% of students tested.

Note: AB = assembly bill; PD = professional development

students for 3 years, to run advisory groups, to plan together, and to develop innovative curriculum ideas. However, there were also many inexperienced, uncredentialed teachers at Robinson when this study began, and teams were uneven in their experience and practice. Experienced Robinson teachers tended to team together, leaving inexperienced teachers in other teams without much veteran support. Robinson students varied widely in their achievement levels, but, on average, student achievement here was also low.

Laurel Ridge, the third school in our sample, was somewhere between the other two in terms of its structure: a number of teaching teams and an advisory period promoted student personalization and provided shared teacher time among teams. Laurel Ridge also boasted a professionally active, generally well-qualified teaching force. Laurel Ridge had long maintained a substantial professional-development agenda and a number of relationships with universities, including attracting many student teachers to its campus. Achievement was average relative to other schools with similar student populations. The strong professional culture at the school was reflected in the fact that teachers there were much more likely to say that they were continually learning, sharing with one another, examining student data, and experimenting with their teaching than teachers at the other schools (see Figure 6.1).

The district-initiated reforms affected the schools in different ways, with the least disruption to Laurel Ridge, a school with already strong capacity, and large impacts on Steward and Robinson. These disruptions were partly structural: For example, Steward became somewhat more personalized for some students with the addition of a sixth-grade cluster and block literacy classes, although it remained the most highly tracked of the three schools. Robinson lost its team and house structure that provided long-term relationships with students. Although the school maintained advisories and introduced Literacy Blocks, at the time we prepared this report there were no longer teams with common preparation periods. While some of the opportunities for strong practice were disrupted by the reform, the reform also dislodged conditions that had created poor practice in other parts of the school. The disruptions were pedagogical and normative: They created major changes in the curriculum and teaching practices as well as new expectations of students and staff.

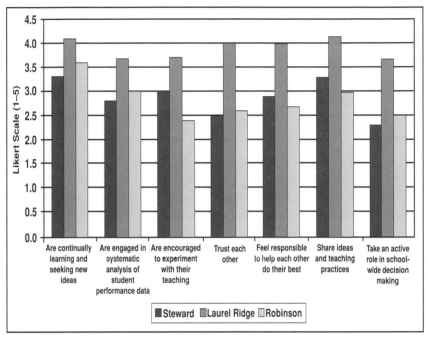

Figure 6.1. *Teachers' Views of Their School's Culture. Q29: To what extent do you agree or disagree with the following statements about the teachers at your school? (Mean rating, by school)*

While district context mediates state policies, school contexts mediate state and district influences (McLaughlin & Talbert, 2001). This "inside-out" analysis confirms that personal and organizational capacity matter, and that school structures, as well as leadership and teacher knowledge, influence the capacity of schools to respond productively to reforms. Our analysis also suggests that San Diego's efforts to improve inadequate practice succeeded in measurable ways; however, there were trade-offs and side effects of the reform process that had yet to be fully addressed by the time we concluded our research. One of these was the increased in-school stratification created by the Literacy-Block classes that were targeted at low-achieving students. Another was the loss of team teaching and planning opportunities in some schools as they bent their structures to implement the new initiatives. We examine these reform effects in three arenas: teacher quality, the literacy initiative, and accountability.

TEACHER QUALITY AND TEACHER DEVELOPMENT

The district's efforts to improve the teaching force had major effects on the availability of qualified teachers within a very short period of time. When our study began in 1998, the three schools' proportions of fully credentialed teachers ranged from 87% (Robinson) to 98% (Laurel Ridge), with the proportion teaching on emergency permits ranging from 11% to 24%[2] (see Table 6.1). In 1998, two of the schools also had a few teachers on intern credentials (the credential issued in California to teachers who are in training while they teach full- or part-time). By 2000, all three schools were staffed by 100% credentialed teachers and the percentage holding emergency permits for any portion of their teaching assignment had declined to 0–3%. These data reflect the fact that the district reduced misassignment of teachers while also recruiting more fully prepared teachers and helping others to complete their training. Some teachers had been evaluated out of teaching at Steward, and all of the schools had peer coaches and stronger professional-development programs with a focus on literacy.

Survey data indicate that more than 90% of the teachers in all three schools were involved in some form of professional development in 2000–2001, although the emphases varied from school to school: teachers at Laurel Ridge were much more likely to be involved in university courses, collaborative research, and teacher networks; those at Robinson were more likely to be involved in peer coaching and observational visits to other schools; and those at Steward were more likely to be involved in workshops. These differences may be associated with teachers' views of their professional development. Teachers at Laurel Ridge were the most positive in their views of the utility of the professional development in which they participated and least likely to say it was "a waste of my time."

Roughly 70% of the beginning teachers from each case-study school were involved in BTSA. This proportion is higher than the proportion of beginning teachers receiving BTSA services statewide (Shields et al., 2001) and is a testament to the district's efforts to scale up the program quickly. At all three schools, BTSA provided structured time for new teachers to get acquainted and opportunities for positive mentee-mentor relationships. Some teachers described their mentoring experiences as very helpful. For example:

[My mentor] spent a lot of time with me. He probably called me at least once a week. I was able to do observations in his classroom. He came by and did observations I think four or five times, and just had real good suggestions. . . . [W]e were focusing on strategies for [English-language] students because I had a sheltered class last year and I had never taught sheltered. . . . And I did some observations of other teachers [in my subject area] at his site who were teaching sheltered. So that was kind of helpful. . . . He facilitated that. He's very good. So I enjoyed working with him.

However, this teacher's experience was not universal. Access to mentors ranged from 21% of beginning teachers in one school to 67% in another. Some novices expressed concern about the match with mentors in terms of content background, school context, or both. In addition to cross-school differences in mentoring opportunities and experiences, we observed differences in the levels of communication about BTSA and the form the support took. Among the areas of complaint was the "paperwork" produced by the state-mandated assessment instrument, CFASST. Said one teacher, "It has . . . potential . . . but it's basically a pain." Whereas elementary teachers generally felt very well served by BTSA, which was well integrated into the literacy reforms they were implementing, many beginning teachers in the middle schools commented on the "busy work," which they felt took too much time from their harried schedules and did not address their immediate needs and concerns.

Steward, a junior high school with 25% beginning teachers (teachers with three or fewer years of experience) provided little formal support to beginning teachers beyond BTSA, although 65% of the new teachers took advantage of opportunities to observe other teachers. Robinson, fighting an uphill battle with teacher turnover, was further taxed by the needs of beginning teachers, who comprised one-third of its teaching staff. Many new teachers did not take advantage of BTSA, citing its demands as too burdensome. Although the principal called together new teachers a few times to talk about their experiences, the peer coach supported individual new teachers, and some experienced teachers occasionally pitched in to help, most Robinson beginning teachers described their first-year experience as "sink or swim." In contrast, Laurel Ridge, a middle school with fewer than 20% beginning teachers, resembled a teaching hospital as it hosted significant numbers of student teachers, their cooperating teachers, and university supervisors. First-year teachers at Laurel were informally looked after by most staff members, had an assigned mentor, experienced peer coaching (46%), attended monthly meetings organized by a vice principal, and reported a high level of supportive communication with administrators and/or department chairs. These differences point to the disparities in capacity among the three schools and how state and district policies play out differently in distinctive contexts.

The experience of Steward teacher David Ruiz, one of three teachers profiled in the next chapter, illustrates the experience of a novice teacher at the most traditionally structured junior high school during the early years of the reform in a school where little teacher collaboration had occurred previously. Despite the fact that he was assigned a BTSA coach in his first year of teaching, Ruiz generally felt isolated and unsupported instructionally. The support provided through the formal coaching relationship was essentially confined to the formal BTSA activities supported by the district. And because his BTSA coach did not teach courses in Ruiz's content area, it was more difficult for him and his coach to connect with respect to content-specific needs. Thus, the district's well-intended efforts to provide high-quality support to beginning teachers fell short for Ruiz. As he noted:

> The whole [BTSA] philosophy is great . . . it just takes time. They gave me a whole bucket of supplies over there. I am sure there is great information and I have talked with my colleagues here (first year teachers) about it, and we all agree. . . . [B]ut I am not going to be able to open that thing up [the BTSA handbook and CFASST portfolio "box"] until summer and really look at it and find out what it is really all about. . . . My BTSA coach is pretty lenient about things . . . and we are supposed to get into that thing and fill out all those forms. It's a pain. I just don't have the time for it. . . . And the idea is . . . when we go to these BTSA meetings they want us to network and feel like we are not alone.

Ruiz's statement reveals his perception that BTSA was for him little more than a social and emotional support network, rather than a means of developing a reflective practice. He received little actual mentoring, and found the box of materials—what the program mostly represented to him—largely inaccessible. In contrast, this elementary principal expressed the predominant view of her colleagues at the elementary level:

> [New teachers] love the BTSA program because it offers them time off to observe other teachers and to go to other schools. And time to spend with a BTSA support provider, who is an experienced mentor teacher, which is outstanding. That is a very popular program. And I make sure that EVERY one of my new teachers is involved in that.

These contrasting views illustrate how a program that is well designed to work at one level of a system can fail to work as well at another. While the literacy focus and training for mentors and other teachers at the elementary school created a strong program focus, the failure to provide time and training for middle school mentors or to match them by content area with their charges created a much less powerful influence at the middle school level. And while a high-capacity school like Laurel Ridge could marshall the intellectual and human resources needed to create its own supports for novices, schools with less capacity were unable to overcome the limitations of the centralized program. The differential capacity across schools was one of the areas most intently targeted by the reform, an area in which, ultimately, much change occurred.

THE LITERACY INITIATIVE

We saw strong evidence of the implementation of SDCS's Literacy Framework at each case-study school, and the district attributed improvements in student reading scores to its literacy-centered reforms. All three schools showed large school-wide gains in reading and language from 1999 to 2001, and additional gains by 2003. Furthermore, in all three cases the gains for Latino students and students of low socioeconomic status were two to four times the state targets for these subgroups between 2002 and 2003 and much steeper than those for other students. Robinson's API score rose more than 80 points between 1999 and 2001, while the school increased the population of students tested from 90% to 100%, and increased another 35 points by 2003. Laurel Ridge experienced steady but somewhat more modest gains (nearly 50 points between 1999 and 2003, while increasing from 93% to 99% of students tested). Steward experienced uneven gains (a drop in 2001 corresponded with the addition of more than 200 students as the school added a sixth grade, but overall gains of nearly 70 points were achieved after a steep increase in 2003 [see Figure 6.2]).

All three case-study schools were influenced by the acquisition or continuation of a principal whose focus was on improving literacy, at least one peer coach position, smaller class sizes and longer class periods for lower-performing sixth- and eighth-grade students, improved classroom libraries, and a greater amount of teacher professional development. Over the 3 years we observed in these schools, students spent more time reading books at their reading level in classrooms that were increasingly designed to support their learning. However, they were doing so in increasingly homogeneous classrooms, since the district's reform strategy placed students according to their reading levels. Teachers more consistently taught reading and writing in a workshop format, shared common terminology for teaching strategies across and within schools, met more frequently with students one-on-one, and made use of multiple measures of student achievement to inform their instruction.

Notwithstanding these changes, middle school teachers did not uniformly embrace these efforts. Some were enthusiastic and engaged

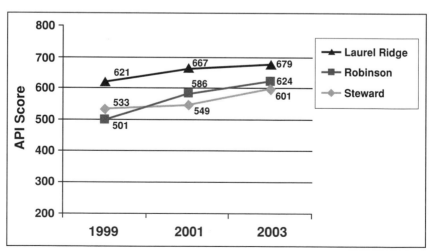

Figure 6.2. *Gains in Academic Performance Index Scores for Sample Middle Schools.*

with the reform; others resented its top-down nature and complained that they were "workshopped to death"; still others remained unclear about teaching expectations. Some teachers described the Literacy Framework as "disjointed." Nevertheless, the framework considerably impacted the culture of teaching at all three schools over the 3 years we observed them. Whereas most teachers had previously taught behind closed doors, more language arts teachers grew accustomed to having peer coaches and administrators in their classrooms on a regular basis, observing one another's teaching practices, and even leading professional-development activities. A peer coach described her work this way:

> Our focus [with yesterday's staff development] was mini-lessons and teachers actually demonstrated mini-lessons that they have done or will be doing in a classroom. I go into the classroom and work with the teachers side-by-side. For example, in one of the classrooms that I went in this morning, the teacher was teaching the kids how to recognize traits of characters . . . she did a mini-lesson . . . and then I assisted in going around and helping to conference with kids as they did their independent reading. . . . I also go in the classroom and do demo lessons. I may go in and do a read-aloud, a shared reading, or a mini-lesson. . . . [But] generally, I will ask them, what is it that you would like for me to observe?

These changes redefined teachers' work in terms of how they related to students, one another, peer coaches, and principled knowledge. Teachers were expected to know their students as readers—through frequent one-to-one meetings with students—and use their knowledge of students' learning needs to guide their instruction. Teachers were encouraged to observe one another, share struggles they encountered with implementing the framework, and discuss such professional books as *Mosaic of Thought* and *Strategies That Work* in relation to their teaching. At each school, some teachers embraced or accepted these new approaches, while others retained more private and autonomous notions of teaching.

While these schools shared much in terms of new experiences around literacy development, they differed in terms of implementation of the Literacy Framework in two important ways: (1) the extent to which schools enacted the Literacy Framework, and (2) the manner in which the reform both intentionally and unintentionally redefined school structures and school culture. School-level implementation of the framework depended on the degree of stability of site principals and peer coaches, the literacy background of site leaders, site teachers' experiences, and the way each school organized opportunities for teacher learning. All three schools underwent significant changes in leadership associated with the reforms over the past 4 years, including at least one change of principal in each school. Previous principals were either dismissed or offered new leadership opportunities, and new principals were recruited because they were perceived to be strong leaders committed to the district's reform agenda. There were noticeable differences across the schools in the knowledge, backgrounds, and working relationships of the principal-peer coach teams, and the ways schools organized time, expertise, and other resources to reach their goals.

Laurel Ridge had the greatest consistency across its literacy classes, and teachers with lower-performing students had common preparation periods and an additional professional-development hour each day to support their instruction. School-wide professional development was led not only by the peer coach, but also by the principal and teachers at the school. Teachers across all subject areas received training in literacy strategies, and many incorporated these strategies in their teaching, although not always comprehensively. Robinson and Steward exhibited less consistency in implementing the framework both across literacy classes and throughout the school.

Steward teachers had less regularly scheduled time set aside to meet with one another than the other schools. Their infrequent meetings were by department. Having relied mainly on consultants and the peer coach for professional development in the past, Steward gradually began to rely more on a few "lead literacy teachers" to design and implement professional development—an arrangement that seemed to support greater distribution of leadership (see, e.g., Spillane, Halverson, & Diamond, 2001) and increased dialogue about instruction among teachers. Steward also acquired a district-provided math administrator devoted to supporting and evaluating math teachers. This addition allowed the principal to spend more time and energy with literacy teachers.

Robinson experienced dramatic restructuring from a previous system of semiautonomous interdisciplinary teams to a more traditional, departmentally organized school. However, teachers continued to have regularly scheduled professional development built into their weekly schedule to learn, plan, and share ideas with one another. Even with the changes, a larger share of teachers at Robinson than at either of the other two schools reported in 2001 that they had common planning with teachers in their subject.[3] Robinson also acquired a math administrator, and was awarded resources from an outside grant to fund a 6:1 teacher-to-coach ratio.[4] These changes expanded coaching opportunities and further impacted the school culture. While many teachers at Robinson bemoaned the loss of their house and team structure and felt as though SDCS had imposed a "one-size-fits-all" structure to achieve its goals for greater equity (as opposed to taking individual school needs or organizational values into account), practice across the school became more consistent. As a function of raising the floor of practice, API score gains in this school were larger than in either of the other two schools, especially for low-achieving students. In fact, by 2001, students of low socioeconomic status performed better at Robinson than low-SES students in either of the other two schools.

By 2002, after considerable dismantling and restructuring had already occurred at the schools, the district not only tolerated but also supported creative school efforts to reestablish some of the elements of personalization for students and collaboration for teachers lost in the adaptations to Literacy Blocks and other requirements, and began to provide individual schools with more flexibility and different supports.

ACCOUNTABILITY

State test-based accountability policies in California were aimed directly at schools, with little acknowledgment of districts, and with rewards or sanctions doled out according to school performance on the SAT-9. However, the district attempted to mediate state accountability policies to ensure that schools' responses to them would not derail the district's current reforms. As we have noted, the state defined accountability much more narrowly than the district or schools in our sample. Closer to the classroom, educators tended to define accountability for results in terms that extended beyond student achievement scores, evaluating success through multiple measures including student participation, behavior, attendance, and myriad formal and informal assessments. Furthermore, San Diego's concept of reciprocal accountability (Elmore, 1996) transcended the "accounting" reflected in test scores with a framework for professional accountability that paid extraordinary attention to who was permitted to work in schools and to the quality of practice those people provided. This more fundamental accountability for professional practice was what the district believed would improve student learning.

While having some common reactions to current state accountability policies, the three schools also had distinctive experiences based on their capacity. All three schools paid attention to the Accountability Performance Index, as parents, teachers, and administrators worry about school ranking and what implications that will have on their reputation, resources, and autonomy. However, principals at all three schools expressed convictions that the state accountability assessment provides only one very limited measure of student success.

Overall, teachers were ambivalent about the testing. While many teachers argued that norm-referenced tests were neither adequate nor accurate means of testing students, most of them agreed that having an assessment that measures students' reading and math proficiency was important. However, many teachers were concerned that the test was not aligned with the state curriculum standards or with good teaching and assessment practice. One math teacher shared this common impression of the impact of the state test:

> Our [school] assessments have been changed by the SAT-9. In math, I am totally against giving multiple choice type questions because I want to see the students' work. If they have the wrong answer, I want to see what they did and help them with that. Math lends itself to that nicely. You can give them partial credit for getting through part of the problem. However, on a multiple choice test, you can't do that. It is either right or wrong. In order to prepare them for the [state assessment], what we have done is made some multiple-choice tests . . . which goes against the grain of how we feel.

So, while teacher-selected assessments (such as "show your work" tests, eighth-grade exit exhibitions, and literacy portfolio entries) are more aligned with teachers' beliefs that students should be tested on what they are expected to learn, the effort and energy required to design, implement, and evaluate these assessments on top of state and district required assessments caused teachers and students to feel pressured and anxious. Some district- and school-wide assessments (e.g., literacy portfolios, student-led conferences), which offered a counterbalance to the SAT-9 and which teachers believe to be worthwhile, were "unmandated," although not eliminated, by the district. This de-emphasis on more performance-oriented school assessments was particularly worrisome to school leaders who insisted that multiple, frequent, and formative assessments were necessary to track student progress and inform instruction.

Ironically, despite noteworthy gains in average API scores and in proportions of students performing in the upper quartiles, each case-study school was at one time identified as an "underperforming" school for failing to meet certain achievement targets on the API. Even Laurel Ridge—a school with large numbers of language minority and low-income students who score above the norm and who experienced substantial gains in both reading and math—saw its API index drop when compared to "similar schools."

There are many anomalies in the calculation of the API that can cause this effect. Other researchers have noted the wide variability in school scores that can be expected from year to year and that make measures like the API and its yearly targets problematic (Kain & Staiger, 2001; Linn & Haug, 2002).[5] An additional issue is that since the API does not take into account test participation rates, schools that test fewer of their English-language learners and special education students can achieve the appearance of higher average performance than similar schools that test more of these students, as San Diego has done.[6] One of the schools had a major change in student population as a grade level was added. Because API scores are not calculated based on the students who have been in a school from one testing to the next, such population changes can depress the index average even if students' scores are increasing.

Another anomaly is that the designation of similar schools includes not only such student demographics as poverty rates but also the proportion of uncertified teachers, a variable that should not be part of the "controls" in the statistical system but rather considered as a strategic input. In practice, what this means is that schools like those in San Diego that reduce the number of uncertified teachers throw themselves into a comparison set with wealthier, more advantaged schools that, in California, generally have high proportions of credentialed teachers. Schools' API scores relative to "similar" schools can be inflated by holding low-performing students out of testing and by hiring uncredentialed teachers—two practices that were virtually eliminated in this district.

By 2003, all of the schools had reached their API targets.[7] Before this occurred, however, each school reacted somewhat differently to the "underperforming" label. Steward teachers expressed a "tell-us-something-we-don't-already-know" attitude, citing daily uphill battles with students and parents. At Robinson, teachers were especially demoralized and "devastated," as one teacher noted, explaining, "Every year they tell us how terrible we are: Title I, Q1/Q2. [They tell us], 'Now do the impossible and make everyone brilliant!'" By contrast, Laurel Ridge teachers voiced concerns mainly with public-relations issues they faced once identified as "low-performing," since their positive reputation in the community was on the line.

These different reactions might be partially explained by teachers' beliefs about standards, accountability, and their own capacities to address them individually or as an entire school. Compared with Laurel Ridge teachers, Steward teachers indicated on a survey that they believed teachers at their school were somewhat less committed to improving student achievement, less likely to believe that standards for student achievement are challenging, attainable, and measurable, less likely to believe that they could significantly affect student achievement by trying different teaching methods, and much less likely to identify their school as having consistent standards from classroom to classroom. Teacher responses from Robinson tended to fall between those at Steward and Laurel Ridge.

Each school also received a grant to develop a plan, facilitated by a state-approved evaluator, to boost student achievement. Despite the district's best efforts to prevent external evaluators from competing with district and school reform goals, these three schools struggled to maintain their focus on district reforms as API goals pressured them to focus on test preparation instead. Individual differences among the evaluators, the nature of the school's original instructional improvement focus, teachers' beliefs and capacity, and the strength of school leadership defined this struggle.

While all the schools received funds from the state, they spent them in different ways. Laurel Ridge and Steward spent money in ways consistent with the district's vision by using the money to support staff development (e.g., additional preparation periods for literacy teachers, time to support teacher observation, coaching opportunities). Robinson, on the other hand, purchased items that were less directly tied to literacy instruction (e.g., school-nurse time, refreshments for students, technology). Taken together, these school comparisons illustrate the tension between locally defined goals and state and district policy.

Nonetheless, there was strong evidence of growing professional accountability in the three schools. We found over time in all of these schools:

1. *Increased professional peer support and collaboration to improve instruction.* Evidence of this includes shared expectations that teachers read professional literature and learn from experts, as well as expectations that teachers share their professional expertise with one another. Teachers increasingly felt support and pressure *from one another* to improve instruction. For example, Laurel Ridge professional-study groups were led by teachers, and many of the groups required teachers to do some professional reading. When a complaint came to the union representative regarding the "requirement to read," she decided to help her colleague understand the importance of meeting this professional expectation rather than grieving it. The principal noted, "The cool thing about it around here is that peer pressure is something that's working for this, because when you go into [teachers'] rooms, for the most part, you can see evidence of professional reading that they've done in an area." Meanwhile, Steward teachers struggling with aspects of their teaching—ranging from general classroom management to the structure of Readers'/Writers' Workshop—began asking for help from other teachers they perceived to be strong. In addition to teacher-to-teacher discussions and in-class coaching, two teachers presented their fellow English department teachers at beginning of 2001–2002 school year with resources and curriculum for Readers'/Writers' Workshop instruction.

2. Greater accountability for teaching through formal and informal observations and evaluations. We saw more informal observations by both administrators and peers, an increased number of teachers documented for ineffective teaching than in years past, and efforts by principals in our study to informally evaluate teachers along a continuum. Most teachers at all of our case-study schools, especially those in math and language arts, experienced more frequent observations by site and district administrators, and some experienced frequent observations by other observers as well (e.g., peers, peer coaches/staff developers, instructional leaders, candidates for administrative positions performing walk-throughs to prove their abilities to critique instruction and articulate next steps for teachers). Many school administrators began to evaluate teachers on a continuum for specific skills to assist staff-development planning. Principals at each of our case-study schools encouraged teachers to develop formal evaluation goals related to student outcomes in literacy. But, as the following exchange between a principal and her instructional leader indicates, teachers may be the ones to suggest learning goals for students and ask the principal to use the formal process of teacher evaluations to hold the teachers accountable.

INSTRUCTIONAL LEADER: What are you holding your teachers accountable for in terms of their progress? I mean, where do you expect those kids to be at the end of the year?

PRINCIPAL: Well, typically, the general thing is that they need to have made at least 2 years of progress in their reading.

IL: Good. Good.

PRINCIPAL: And you know what? The teachers decided. The Literacy Block teachers are the ones who told me that they thought that would be a good goal.

IL: Good! Excellent.

PRINCIPAL: And some of them have written them into their [teacher evaluations].

IL: Excellent. . . .

PRINCIPAL: Well, you can't just make 1 year of progress, and I think 2 years is minimal.

One of our case-study principals noted:

> I think I did a much better job evaluating people this year. Part of it is be-
> cause I know more about language arts. . . . And so, of course, now that
> I know more, I'm able to provide them with a little more feedback then
> I could last year. . . . The way I do principaling at a school will never be
> the same. . . . Because what we're doing is really important work that im-
> pacts kids' lives. We weren't in classrooms before. . . . No one ever came
> in my room even when I was [a teacher being evaluated]. So I think that's
> one of the reasons that's been hard for older teachers to change. So all of
> the training I've gotten, and Tony's [Alvarado's] position around kids
> and the needs of our kids and our responsibilities as educators, all the
> discussions around professionalism. I'm not just a manager of an opera-
> tion, but I have the instructional piece and the accountability piece that
> is more important than the operational piece.

3. *Use of student data to hold teachers accountable for their teaching.*
The use of data is yet another element in increasing professional accountability. In some cases it involves teachers evaluating student work
against a performance rubric, in accordance with district or state content
standards. We observed this practice in our case-study schools. All three
principals met with teachers in some capacity to review student reading
levels. During the 2001–2002 school year, the Laurel Ridge principal required language arts teachers to track student reading levels according to
the books they were reading while she provided teachers with SDRT and
SAT-9 reading score data. The principal provided teachers with an analysis of their students' SDRT data, sharing with them reading level improvements by class, by group as applicable (for example, grade level,
English Language Learners, Gifted and Talented Education [GATE]),
and by individual students. At Robinson, the principal met individually
with teachers after comparing student data herself and providing comparison scores (SDRT scores from 2000 with those of 2001) for students
with matched data. At Steward, the principal provided student test score
data to teachers for the first time in 2001–2002, explaining that she
would discuss student scores with them, help them reflect on their teaching practice, and figure out ways to support struggling students. In addition, we saw a prevailing expectation that teachers use standards to guide
their instruction and evaluation of students. Furthermore, in a growing

number of classrooms we saw responses to the district's emphasis on assessing where students are in order to plan how to get them to standard, rather than merely teaching the content standards as outlined in the state framework.

4. *A growing sense of principal accountability to other principals*. In formal or structured settings—such as principal conferences, walkthroughs scheduled to include peers, meetings between coaching principals and their mentees—principals discussed professional reading, observed one another's videotaped staff conferences and critiqued them, shared their schools' instructional needs and professional-development priorities, and examined their efforts to evaluate teachers. Informally, principals formed their own book clubs, visited one another's schools, and talked and provided support to one another. One principal noted:

> I would say that informal relationship[s with other principals is where I seek support]. And also, interestingly enough, the middle level principals—a portion of that group—are a strong support. I am thinking about [one principal who] said [this summer], "You know I am having a difficult time finding time to read *Non-Fiction Matters* and think about it in some kind of constructive way. Maybe if we get together a little and make ourselves do it, that would be beneficial." And I said, "Sign me up!" because I'm experiencing the same thing. . . . I felt more obligated to do it for my colleagues. I knew I needed to do it for myself, too, for the learning community. It really provided the real world opportunity to do that.

Gradually, as communities of learners came together both within and across schools, among teachers and principals, a sense of capacity grew, fueled in part by a sense of common cause.

NOTES

1. The names of all schools and teachers in our study are pseudonyms.

2. Some emergency permits are held by teachers who are fully credentialed in one field but are working out of their credential field for part or all of their current assignment.

3. Our teacher survey data revealed that 40% of Robinson teachers reported having common planning time with teachers in their subject, while fewer than 30% of Laurel Ridge and Steward teachers did.

4. This compares with Laurel Ridge at 50:1 and Steward at roughly 30:1.

5. Kentucky's similar accountability index, which produced schools that boomeranged from "rewards" status one year to "sanctions" the next, was repealed the year before California's was enacted.

6. Although schools must test a certain proportion of students to be eligible for cash bonuses, the API index does not factor in test participation rates in deriving API scores.

7. Even as all of the schools reached their state API targets, two of three failed to make "adequate yearly progress" on the federal No Child Left Behind standards because, even though previously low-scoring Latino and low-income students made huge gains, their more advantaged and higher-scoring white or Asian students did not make comparable gains.

CHAPTER 7

The Teachers' View: Where Reform Hits the Road

In any reform initiative, what really matters for students is what happens inside the classroom, "where reform hits the road." This chapter tells the story of three teachers from the middle schools we have just discussed, and how their work and learning were influenced by the system-wide changes. David Ruiz, a young beginning social studies teacher, launched his teaching career at Steward Junior High just as the district-wide reform was getting underway. Leanne Murray, with nearly 10 years of experience teaching in teams, was at that time entering her sixth year of teaching social studies and language arts at Robinson Middle School. Finally, Nancy Ogden, a "teaching-assistant-turned-teacher" and self-described "late bloomer," had taught English and social studies at Laurel Ridge Middle School for 8 years. While these three teachers certainly do not represent all of the nearly 7,400 classroom teachers in SDCS, their stories illustrate how individual teachers experienced changes in their practice and professional learning in the 3-year period from 1998 to 2001.

Quite often, research suggests, sweeping reform efforts have been important and visible in board decisions, central-office structures, and formal policy changes, but have had few effects on what teachers actually do. Larry Cuban (1984) likens education policies to storms that merely touch the ocean's surface, unable to penetrate classroom teaching practice that resides deep near the ocean's floor:

> The surface is agitated and turbulent, while the ocean floor is calm and serene (if a bit murky). Policy churns dramatically, creating the appearance of major changes, calculated to reinforce the symbolic rewards of

action for policymakers and to cement the logic of confidence in the institutions, while deep below the surface, life goes on largely uninterrupted.

These teacher cases, however, suggest that the systemic reform in SDSC dove below the surface, propelled by a clear conception of powerful instruction and a theory of how to build teacher capacity to ensure every student received such teaching. Our data about the teachers came from interviews (at least four per teacher), classroom observations (at least four classes per teacher), observations of professional-development activities in which the teachers participated (e.g., staff meetings, department meetings, site-based workshops), and artifacts of their students' work.

Mirroring the findings from our district-wide surveys, all of the case-study teachers expressed beliefs that all students can learn to high standards, and all took responsibility for knowing their students as learners in order to teach them specific knowledge and skills. All three teachers clearly strove to know their students, master their content, and develop and improve upon an array of teaching strategies. Beyond these commonalities, the teachers carried out the district's vision for instructional improvement in different ways. The extent to which the teachers applied their professional knowledge to the individual needs of students varied, as did the teachers' instructional priorities. Teachers' experiences with district reforms reflected not only their individual differences, but also variations associated with their schools. We observed differences in the type and amount of resources available to each teacher (e.g., time, space, money, structures) and in the teachers' professional community at each of the schools. These factors affected the degree to which the teachers had the opportunity to reflect upon and refine their practice in communal settings.

Nevertheless, we found the emergence of a common language about instruction across and within schools, as well as greater professional accountability demands for both individuals and groups of educators. By 2001, all of these teachers worked among a group of more qualified teachers than they had 3 years earlier. Furthermore, the district's literacy focus influenced whom each teacher was teaching, what she taught, and how. Each participated in a more public teaching practice—in planning, teaching, and reflecting. Finally, each participated in professional development that was more unified and coherent than in years past. Each of the teachers encountered more stratified groups of students, was adjusting to new professional roles, and expressed both appreciation for and frustration with aspects of the reform. Consideration of these commonalities and differences provides some useful insights into how a rapidly implemented systemic reform affects teachers who are, in many ways, its major targets.

DAVID RUIZ—STEWARD JUNIOR HIGH SCHOOL

David Ruiz is a young teacher who began teaching right after he graduated from college with a credential to teach secondary social studies. At the time of this study, he taught world studies/geography to seventh and ninth graders, and most of his students were English-language learners. He began his full-time position at Steward Junior High School after a few months as a long-term substitute teacher for English as a Second Language (ESL) classes in 1999. Ruiz was dedicated to his students and passionate about helping them reach their potential. It is fair to say that Steward did not entirely fulfill Ruiz's vision of a supportive teaching and learning environment, but that it embodied some of his goals for his own teaching contribution:

> It all comes down to my whole philosophy as a teacher. I want to allow my students to be independent thinkers, to think about their role, and think about themselves. I want them to have a role in their own education. . . . I expect them to work hard, and to be respectful, and to come in here and take it seriously. I heard that [Steward] didn't have a good reputation a few years ago, and part of the reason I wanted to work here was because I feel like [Steward] is in a transition. Every school has its bad elements, but I really feel . . . that there is so much potential in some of these kids. . . . Some of these kids are so intelligent and they have what we call the "ganas"—they really want it, they have the desire.

The term "transition" was, perhaps, an understatement. Between 1999 and 2001, the school experienced three principals (two permanent and one interim), four vice principals, three peer coaches, and a nearly

60% turnover in teaching staff. The district placed significant pressures on Steward, as with other schools throughout the district, to improve student achievement and end its participation in the state's Immediate Intervention for Underperforming Schools Program (II/USP). District supports included: assigning to the school a principal who was supportive of the district's reform effort and capable of organizing the school around instructional reform; providing funding for such positions as a peer coach and math administrator; allocating money to develop classroom libraries; and furnishing some discretionary funding for the school to meet instructional needs (e.g., paying for curriculum consultants).

Ruiz experienced notable changes at the school during his early years of teaching, both in terms of professional support and classroom practice. In his first year of teaching, he commented that the culture of Steward did not foster professional collaboration. In general, he did not have many opportunities in the regular course of the day to plan with other teachers, and he received less support than he expected as a new teacher:

> [I] mainly worked alone . . . I've also been with other teachers who have not been so helpful, which is really surprising, because I thought it was going to be more democratic . . . you know, where teachers help each other out. . . . I have noticed that some teachers are very, very personal about keeping their materials to themselves . . . I was surprised that some people were not as friendly as I would expect.

However, after his first year of teaching, as the school began to change, Ruiz had more opportunities to work and reflect with other professionals on instructional matters. In the summer of 2001, Ruiz worked with a colleague and consultant to develop curriculum for his seventh-grade social studies classes, incorporating many of the district's emphasized literacy strategies. Specifically, he narrowed his social studies content to make room for teaching specific literacy strategies including: (1) learning nonfiction text features; (2) "determining importance" of text; (3) using "questioning" as a strategy to help students comprehend text; and (4) supporting students' writing of paragraphs. The teacher he worked with noted: "We really figured out that whatever we did to support literacy in history would actually end up helping us in the end—because if they're stronger readers they can do more independent work, they can determine importance [of a text] on their own." Throughout the year, the consultant observed the team's teaching, and fostered critical feedback sessions around whether the lessons were a reflection of what the teachers had planned for them to be.

Within the school, Ruiz observed a highly respected Genre Studies teacher on staff. In spring 2002, Ruiz joined a few department colleagues, his principal, and vice principal in visiting Laurel Ridge to observe social studies teachers who incorporated literacy strategies in their curriculum. Organized by administrators at both schools, this trip offered the Steward teachers some ideas for using elements of the literacy framework in their classrooms. They observed that Laurel Ridge teachers were open to trying new ways of blending social studies content with literacy strategies. While the Laurel Ridge teachers did not offer perfectly integrated lessons, they provided Steward social studies teachers with a glimpse of how a faculty committed to supporting literacy instruction across all disciplines enacted that vision.

Support for Ruiz to develop a more public, reflective practice accommodating the Literacy Framework included funding, professional development, and an emerging network of professionals. Ruiz received money to buy books for his classroom library, and he used this funding to purchase "high-interest" books related to topics covered in his curriculum. The school-wide instructional focus in 2001–2002 on "purposeful planning" and ongoing efforts to learn more about students and their efforts to make meaning from text supported both teacher and student learning. Professional development in study groups helped Ruiz build relationships with other colleagues rooted in observations of, discussions about, and planning for instruction.

Although Ruiz's opportunities expanded so that he was able to work with talented peers at his school and beyond, there were shortcomings in the structure at Steward that limited more consistent work with peers. Most of the "now and then" collaboration he experienced with school-site colleagues lacked continuity and depth; this was a function of time and organizational and cultural constraints. While the principal was able to coordinate common preparation periods for some groups of teachers to share their work, she was unable to grant Ruiz a common preparation period with other seventh-grade social studies teachers in 2001–2002. This major change in the culture and organization of Steward could not immediately be implemented school-wide. Thus, while he exchanged resources and lessons with his colleagues via their school mailboxes, Ruiz had little opportunity to exchange ideas and information about students during the regular course of his workday. Brief chance encounters with teachers who had students in common with Ruiz failed to ensure that students received adequate attention.

Professional development at Steward became much more coherent over the 3 years, but administrators still struggled with supporting teacher learning to a meaningful depth. Staff meetings and department meetings, held once a month after school, offered little time to focus on instruction. All-day staff meetings, which allowed for rich discussions, occurred sporadically throughout the school year. And while administrators increasingly leveraged the teacher-evaluation process to support teacher learning, Ruiz experienced the process only every other year once he had tenure. Besides the time constraints and challenges to providing coherent, deep professional development, another obstacle for Ruiz was the absence of a community of teachers devoted to reflecting on and improving their classroom practice. There were only one or two teachers with whom he shared ideas about instruction in his content area. The process of fostering new professional norms that required a major cultural shift was slow.

Nevertheless, the professional community at Steward clearly underwent change from a culture dominated by independence to one that was increasingly public and open. Among some groups of teachers, camaraderie expanded into collegiality, despite the fact that a number of staff members resented changing expectations and distrusted district and site administrators.

This evolution occurred sooner in some departments than others. Accountability pressures that prioritized language arts and mathematics skills at both the state and district levels forced other subject areas to "wait in line" for all kinds of resources—the district's reform concentrated on literacy first as a "gateway" to supporting all other subjects. And while the district purported to hold all teachers accountable for incorporating reading strategies into their classroom instruction, principals, peer coaches, and literacy and math administrators were so busy addressing the needs of language arts and math teachers that other teachers, social studies teachers among them, were often left to fend for themselves. Ruiz experienced fewer classroom observers and less intensive professional development than his language arts peers. As a consequence, he relied mainly on himself to develop his curriculum and reflect on his teaching. Like 96% of the teachers in our district survey who reported attending workshops, conferences or trainings, and 30% who reported taking additional university courses, Ruiz participated in professional development beyond his school, enrolling in university courses, attending district workshops, and scoring student portfolios.[1] While motivated to gain experiences directly tied to supporting his students, he also sought to make himself more versatile on the job market and advance himself on the salary schedule.

With the modest support he received, Ruiz exhibited changes in his teaching that reflected the district's vision for classroom instruction. First, by 2001 he had incorporated several aspects of the Readers'/Writers' Workshop format into his classroom. Besides developing a "mini-lesson" tied to a standard, he offered his students time for independent work. He coached his students in sharing their ideas with one another in verbal and written form, and gave them extended periods of time to do so. In addition, Ruiz and his students frequently referred to student-generated charts posted on the classroom walls as they learned and compared historical eras. Furthermore, Ruiz took care in selecting student work, along with his own, to model what he wanted students to do. He endeavored to plan instruction based on student needs, and he sought better materials to support his efforts.

David Ruiz's experiences identify some benefits and challenges of building capacity for new ways of teaching. While the improvements at Steward began to pay off in strengthened instruction, it is clear that reform comes slowly in schools with few initial structures and little tradition of supporting collegial learning. Steward's situation demonstrated how important it is for reformers to focus on school structures (creating time and teams for collaboration around students and subject matter, for example) as much as on instructional expertise building. Furthermore, a tightly focused reform like the one pursued in San Diego will not influence practice in all subject areas for all teachers with equal force. The district's efforts to provide stronger leadership for

Steward were beginning to show in a number of ways, as we described in the previous chapter. The challenge for systemic reformers is how to allocate limited resources and attention to ensure focus and progress in core instructional areas while also changing the leadership and design of schools that have been dysfunctional in the past, and investing in teachers across content areas. The challenge for teachers like David Ruiz is how to continue to build their skills and maintain commitment to a site that serves students who deserve their care while the system is catching up to the students' individual and collective needs.

LEANNE MURRAY—ROBINSON MIDDLE SCHOOL

Leanne Murray, in her tenth year of teaching language arts and social studies, experienced the San Diego City Schools district reform in a different and dramatic way. Of the three case-study teachers, Murray was the most motivated to learn the Literacy Framework and implement it in her classroom. However, the implementation of the framework also collided with the collegial structures that had supported her at Robinson. The reform, as it encountered her school context, brought out both the best and worst in Murray's teaching, and it posed a number of dilemmas for her as an individual and her school community as a whole. Whereas Steward had been a traditional junior high school with a factory-model schedule and departmentalized structure, Robinson Middle School had been an alternative school featuring interdisciplinary teams that worked with a shared group of students over multiple years. The reform had very different initial impacts in the different schools.

Murray had come to Robinson from another school with a cadre of teachers who shared a common teaching philosophy, and Robinson's team structure afforded them considerable autonomy. Like other teachers at the school, Murray and her teammates had a common preparation period each day; this allowed them to develop their curriculum, discuss individual students, determine which students would be assigned to what teachers when and for how long, analyze student progress, and conference with students and parents. Furthermore, because school let out early each Wednesday for staff development, teachers had more time to meet with one another in groups as teams, departments, or as an entire faculty.

As we noted in chapter 6, this structure supported some very strong teams of senior teachers, like Murray's, but it also left isolated and un-mentored some weak teams of less skilled and less experienced teachers.

Before her introduction to the district's curricular reforms, Murray's instruction was heavily influenced by the common planning of her team, organized around interdisciplinary themes, and guided by the district and state content-area standards. About standards, Murray said, "We definitely are mindful of the standards. Standards are important to us and guide us, because we want to make sure that the kids are prepared to go on to the next level and that there's some rhyme and reason to the process."

All the teachers in her team assumed all students could learn, and took seriously their job to support that learning. They agreed with Murray that "We need to learn how to reach them . . . and this is the challenge which makes it interesting." The district reform did not disrupt this structure for the first couple of years. Together the team reviewed student data (test scores, reading levels, etc.), which helped the teachers determine student needs that in turn guided their instruction. Furthermore, Murray, along with her colleagues, maintained clear and high expectations for student work, taught students metacognitive skills, and led activities and assignments supportive of students' continual reflection on their learning. One of Murray's students said, "We get to do things on our own, like this. We get to be independent learners." Murray employed numerous activities to engage students' interest, access their prior knowledge, and assess what they learned from their classroom experiences. For example, using "Maya Quest"—an online interdisciplinary inquiry into the life of the Mayan people—Murray facilitated students' explorations and assessed their learning through a notebook they assembled. Knowing what students were studying in their other subjects, she fostered connections across disciplines; and culminating interdisciplinary projects and field trips were ways Murray and her colleagues encouraged students to synthesize their learning across core subject areas and develop their creative talents. In addition, Murray often led and participated in a host of school-wide events that strengthened school-home connections.

Murray encountered the district's Literacy Framework while thriving in her interdisciplinary team. As a person who actively pursued professional development to further her teaching and who believed in collaborating with other teachers on issues of instruction, she embraced the Readers'/Writers' Workshop and applied for the position of peer coach/staff developer at Robinson. Attending many district workshops throughout the year and during the summer as well as in-school staff development and reading a host of professional books (including those facilitated through school-based book-study groups), Murray demonstrated her eagerness to absorb what she could about teaching young people to read and write. Of the Literacy Framework, she stated:

> I don't have a problem with the workshop model, I love the workshop model . . . it's just good pedagogy, it just makes sense. It works, and it makes sense. There are realities to contend with: you know, class size, management, record keeping kinds of stuff are real issues. But that's not something wrong with the workshop model.

With the literacy reforms, Murray's classroom became more student-centered. She adopted the Readers'/Writers' Workshop (RWW) model, teaching whole-class or small-group lessons in reading or writing based more on her students' learning needs. She determined these needs through one-on-one conferences with students, her analysis of student work and achievement scores, and students' reflections on their learning. We observed that after a group lesson, students had independent time to practice what Murray asked them to do. During this time, Murray had the opportunity to meet with a small group requiring more support, or to check in with individual students to inform her next steps.

Murray's classroom included an area where students congregated for common lessons. Students could see their work exhibited throughout the room, and charts from classroom work were posted throughout the room to remind students what they had been working on and to prompt them as needed. As called for by the Literacy Framework, the students' reading diet was largely comprised of trade books written at their reading level, and Murray taught students particular reading strategies (e.g., visualization, questioning, predicting, developing vocabulary, etc.) to help them make meaning from text. She integrated previously successful teaching strategies (e.g., interactive notebook) as she tried new ways of teaching with the RWW format.

Murray faced what she describes as her worst teaching situation in 2001–2002 after the resources she had thrived on and relied upon in an interdisciplinary teaching team completely dissolved to accommodate the district-mandated Literacy Block. She had been one of four teachers in a sixth-grade team empowered to make decisions about curriculum, schedules, student supports, and resource allocation. Her teaching team, along with its common preparation period, was eliminated. Gone were the students she had in common with colleagues; gone with that were opportunities to schedule students for special classroom experiences; and gone were the opportunities to plan interdisciplinary units with her colleagues and maintain a tight community of students in a "family-like" environment. While the school maintained its half-day staff-development time each week, Murray lost key structural supports she identified as influencing and enhancing her instructional practice. During a particularly frustrating time, she reflected on the decision to eliminate school teams:

> There is no team at all. So . . . what we've gone to, we meet as grade levels and departments. . . . The school made a decision that teams were out. . . . It was an administrative decision. . . . Our understanding is that Bersin, that the Institute, does not like teams. What I've been told is that there is one way to do things, the Institute way, the Bersin way, and that's not part of it. Teaming is not appropriate. . . . [M]y cynical belief is that it undermines power. You don't want teachers to be empowered. If they're empowered, then they're going to think that they know something; and if they think they know something, they're going to want to be creative; and creativity is not in vogue right now—you follow the framework.

While the district's reform model philosophically argued that teachers should be empowered to solve problems, Murray's experience caused her to doubt the district's sincerity. In fact, she took the opposite message to be true—she believed teachers were discouraged to solve problems in ways they saw fit. The centralizing force of the district-office approach collided with the decentralized power of Robinson's school team structures.

During her most frustrating year of teaching, Murray was invited to be a literacy coach who teaches part-time and supports other staff members part-time. This position was funded by an outside foundation through a grant to three middle schools to provide a coach-to-teacher ratio of 6:1. She accepted the position. So, although losing the previous school structures limited her ability to team with other teachers in what used to be a more distinctive "school within a school," Murray became part of an enhanced model of the SDCS reform. She became a peer coach in a way that did not require her to leave the classroom; this approach gave her a potentially more effective model of working with other teachers, being able to demonstrate instruction in an authentic classroom setting. Murray described her role as a model teacher/coach as being able to stay connected with teaching while "figuring out how to mediate the Blueprint, how to apply it, how to sift through it, how to make it real in our classrooms . . . so we act as a basic kind of filter and we address and support new teachers and their needs."

Murray's experience reflected the district's efforts to establish and expand professional accountability throughout the entire system. Whereas she had held herself and her tight-knit group of colleagues accountable for the learning of their team's students in years past, Murray became a key player in a broader kind of accountability—one extending from her team to her entire school and district. Despite losing students and time in common with a small group of teachers, Murray was now able to avail herself of time and structures supporting a reflective school-wide and district-wide dialogue about instruction. She met informally with other teachers as well. She reported about her experience as a coach, "We made lots of observations over the last year about our lowest achievers, what commonalities we see, and what are some ways that we might address those weaknesses."

Murray's teaching became more public and open to critique over the years of the initial reform. Besides having numerous visits from the principal, peer coach, instructional leader, and others, she participated in small study groups of teachers. In these groups, which were facilitated by her school principal, consultants, and a peer coach/staff developer, Murray not only shared her ideas about teaching in discussions, but she also observed and critiqued others' teaching while others did the same for her. School-wide professional development also focused on the Literacy Framework along with the principal's school-wide focus of increasing "Accountable Talk" one year. In addition, in small groups some teachers read and discussed books about pedagogy.

Leanne Murray's case illustrates some of the challenges and dilemmas facing the school and district reform efforts and shows how micro and macro tensions exist even within a school. While Murray's team functioned at a high level, promoting a cycle of improving instruction among a small group of experienced teachers, other teams in the school were dysfunctional. Teams entirely comprised of beginning teachers lacked the support and capacity to use resources available to them in the school structure. Other teams had members who were simply unwilling to work together, despite the capacity to do so. In the end, the district's goals for enhancing the professional community throughout the entire school overrode the small group's desires to maintain the structures they had used to strengthen their teaching and learning community.

Leanne Murray's case also illustrates some potentially unforeseen costs exacted by the reforms. Murray's team lost a valuable teacher community, and with it a tight-knit teacher-student community. She and her colleagues had adeptly used the advisory period, flexible schedules, and a common preparation period to support a highly personalized environment for students. They knew not only a lot about the personal circumstances of each student, but also a great deal about them as learners. And, while the advisory period survived the dismantling of teams at Robinson, opportunities for teachers to share insights about students were significantly curtailed. The district's own vision of effective instruction was predicated on knowing students well, and research supports the value of that position (Darling-Hammond, 1997b; Resnick & Hall, 1998). How, then, might a district signal support for structures that maintain or improve personalization amidst other reform goals? How might leaders engaged in systemic reform initiatives from the top of a system consider the different potential needs of schools based on the schools' existing structures, strengths, and shortcomings?

NANCY OGDEN—LAUREL RIDGE MIDDLE SCHOOL

Nancy Ogden, an eighth-grade language arts and social studies teacher at Laurel Ridge Middle School, had been teaching for over 10 years when the San Diego reform was launched. Teachers at Laurel Ridge long had a reputation for being very professional and were noted for continuing their own education in various ways: getting master's degrees, taking additional coursework for supplements, or seeking professional workshops for their own improvement. Ogden fit this description well: within the past 10 years she had earned a Gifted and Talented Education (GATE) supplemental credential, completed coursework to fulfill the school board's requirements for CLAD credentials (for teaching culturally and linguistically diverse learners), and completed much of the coursework toward a master's degree. In addition, she had read professional books to enhance her teaching, as well as a bounty of adolescent literature.

As we talked with and observed her over the course of 3 years, Ogden seemed increasingly reflective about her students, considering what they knew and how to best engage and support them as learners. She incorporated many aspects of the Literacy Framework into her teaching, became more accustomed and open to others' critiques of her teaching, and became involved in more directly co-constructing knowledge about teaching with her peers.

Ogden entered the teaching profession after she had begun her family, worked as a teaching assistant for 10 years, and tried other professional routes before she acknowledged, "My love is teaching; what am I waiting for?" She was passionate about treating all students as individuals, providing them with new experiences, and connecting them with the world. She was an enthusiastic learner who could identify with struggles her students might have, a fact she shared with them in part to help them feel more comfortable asking questions and seeking clarification. She shared her goals as a teacher:

> I want students to be self-motivated. They need to have good self-esteem and be comfortable; I also think they should be accountable for standards . . . I believe that we need to help encourage students to have a goal and thirst for learning . . . to be responsible citizen[s]. . . . I want children to have a love for literature. I want them to enjoy writing.

For most of her teaching career, Ogden worked closely with two other teachers sharing roughly 100 eighth-grade students. The team created a community among students and teachers, and it allowed the teachers to develop an integrated curriculum across three subject areas. During an interdisciplinary unit covering Lewis and Clark's expedition of the Louisiana Purchase, for example, students read Scott O'Dell's *Streams to the River, River to the Sea* while studying plant and animal classification. Ogden shared how team teachers and students benefited from their collaboration:

> Team support. We feed off each other; we say, "Ok, here's a topic. What can we do?" And you take that topic and you can just go with it, get ideas, brainstorm, you don't feel like you're out there struggling, trying to stay afloat. And . . . discipline is not a problem. . . . So we have a common prep, which is period five, we'll pull the student in during our prep period and sit down with the student. . . . And it's very powerful for meeting at a table with three teachers . . . and generally, we can handle our problem right there at the table.

Ogden voiced her belief that students need to be challenged with high expectations, not only in their work but also in their social behavior. She placed written expectations for the class on the front board, and she explained that many of her curriculum decisions were influenced by the demands students face in high school. Like most teachers at her school, Ogden indicated that standards strongly influenced her decisions about instructional content, pedagogy, and assessments. Our classroom observations confirmed that she was consistent about connecting what she taught with specific standards. As she rattled off several of the standards by number and quoted specific language from the standards, there was no doubt she had internalized them and used them to plan. She was also keenly aware of student diversity:

> Teachers need to be held accountable, and they need to be aware. I think the standards help keep teachers focused on what they should be teaching students. . . . Generally, I am all for ways that we can hold students accountable for their learning. There are tensions though. I have students who range (in their reading) from the second grade to college level. And I have 12 students who read and write at the K–3 level.

Ogden was convinced that students learn better when what they are learning is connected to their own experiences in some way. This was evident from many of the assignments she gave her students. For example, she asked students to identify experiences in their own lives that might reflect the experience of a character in the book they were reading. In another example, she helped students learn the concept of "plurality" by relating it to the class's demographics before describing it in the historical context they were studying.

Ogden consistently modeled to both her students and her peers what it means to be a learner. She looked critically at her own work and sought ways she might improve her lessons so students would be successful. She described her self-assessment process in this way, "You see, if it's not working, why is it not working? What do I have to do? So, it's teacher assessment and reevaluation. . . . It's never just taking a lesson out and saying, we just did this 10 years ago, let's do it again. It doesn't work that way."

Increasingly, student data influenced what Ogden taught. In previous years, she had examined student work for the district-mandated eighth-grade writing portfolio, taking cues from that work about what she needed to teach to support students "getting to standard." Rather than a grammar book, mistakes Ogden noted in her students' writing assignments dictated her grammar lessons. More recently, she and other teachers had examined students' scores on standardized tests. In 2001–2002, the district's expectation that teachers "know their students as readers" led Ogden's principal to require language arts teachers to track students' independent reading books. Analysis of these data revealed how well reading levels of the books corresponded to students' reading scores, and informed Ogden and others as they planned individual, small-group, and whole-class instruction.

Ogden had school-level supports to assist her in knowing students well: her interdisciplinary team, advisory period, professional development emphasizing student needs and student engagement, and the formal teacher-evaluation process, to name a few. As teacher evaluation was refined in the district, it became more helpful. For example, after a classroom observation, Ogden's principal encouraged her to give students more time to work on their own or with one another on learning tasks. Speaking of the formal evaluation conducted by the principal, Ogden said:

> But I learned something from her evaluation, because even though I was changing activities all the time and moving quickly and moving smoothly, I didn't devote enough time in my mind to the students' hands-on actually working. And I could see that from her printout. . . . If she

had said to me, "How'd your lesson go?" I would have said, "Fantastic." But then when I saw three minutes for this, four minutes for that, and I saw it broken down. . . . But, you know what? If I had to do this over again, I would probably get rid of some parts and get more time for student work. And I wouldn't have known it [without her observation notes].

For her 2000–2001 evaluation, in which she and the principal had agreed on a goal for the year, Ogden selected five students for whom she cultivated greater home-school communication. Through e-mails with parents and students, weekly meetings with one parent, and frequent phone calls, she stayed in close contact with her students and students' parents throughout the year. She felt that support had had a positive influence on her students, and said, "I wish I could do that for all of my students."

In terms of teaching, Ogden adopted the RWW model in her English classes, read multiple professional texts to support her implementation of the district's framework, and even modeled particular strategies for her peers at staff-development workshops.

And on the positive side we've gotten a lot of training for in-services and instruction from our principal [and our] staff developer of what the [Readers'/Writers'] Workshop looks like, what Accountable Talk looks like. . . . So I think it has made us aware of what we are supposed to be doing, and this is what the administrators want to see, this is the big push from the district . . . it's very clear what we're supposed to be doing, how we're supposed to be doing it with modeling and questions.

Beginning in 2000–2001, the principal and peer coach at Laurel Ridge supported small-scale professional-development study groups. In 2001–2002 the study groups, comprised of about 12 teachers each, were arranged by theme (e.g., Readers'/Writers' Workshop, technology, differentiation of instruction, use of assessment to drive instruction). They focused on one or more reading strategies that teachers agreed upon as a group; read at least one professional book related to their theme and/or strategy; and discussed, planned, demonstrated, and critiqued lessons focused on their study group interest.

Ogden participated in the adolescent literature group. Three times over the course of the year, her group read a young adult novel, discussed ways to enhance student comprehension of the text[2] using literacy strategies, observed a "lead" teacher demonstrate a lesson, and met to debrief the lesson. After each cycle, group members were expected to develop their own lesson, teach it, and reflect on it with the group. Meeting after school and during minimum-day and full-day professional sessions, teachers had ample time to discuss, observe, and reflect on their ideas and work. Furthermore, the continuity of theme throughout the year allowed teachers to build on what they were learning from others. Despite these strengths, observations of Ogden's study group revealed that teachers were struggling to transition from supporting one another emotionally to supporting one another in more substantive and critical ways. Furthermore, the role of student-learning needs in driving decisions about "what to teach and how" was still a new, relatively undeveloped idea in the study group. In the principal's view, this was the next horizon for the professional-development work in this school. The peer coach and principal's mantra was, "When you decide your students need to know such-and-such, how is it that you determine that is what they need?" They prodded teachers for evidence of their observations and diagnoses of student needs.

Nancy Ogden felt that the peer coach assigned to Laurel Ridge supported her growth in practice. Ogden noted in the 2000–2001 school year:

> Well, I was on the committee who hired [the peer coach]. She is young, energetic, knowledgeable, and she has leadership qualities, but she is not pushy. She really encouraged me in a gentle way to start using some of the reading strategies. It's hard teaching the [Readers'/Writers' Workshop] format in one hour with the eighth graders. [Other teachers have] the two hour block, but I am doing it in just under one hour. But the support is good.

Despite Ogden's willingness to try out new practices, she initially harbored some resentment toward the district's reforms and their potential threat to structures and resources that had supported her own teaching and learning. Specifically, she feared that her opportunity to work with other teachers in an interdisciplinary team would be wiped out as Literacy Block classes impinged upon master-schedule planning, and she worried that she would suffer larger class sizes while the class sizes of two-hour blocks were kept low. As it turned out, school-level decisions around the master schedule preserved the interdisciplinary team, and Ogden was able to continue teaching in what she felt was a nearly ideal situation. Her fears about larger class sizes were realized, however; and she lost heterogeneity in the composition of her one-hour language arts classes because of the tracking of lower readers into Literacy Block classes.

Because of the district reform and the supports and expectations it embodied, Ogden was pushed to make her work more public in different ways than she had experienced before. She learned new strategies for accomplishing her deeply held commitment to student learning. Her case, and that of her school, illustrates that while the district reform has done much to increase school-wide professional accountability, transforming a school culture from one of congeniality to collegiality is difficult work. It also suggests that maintaining locally defined goals in the face of district or state policies—in this case preserving the interdisciplinary teaching team—was possible. However, the consequence of moving lower-performing students out of the interdisciplinary team was less student diversity in the team and restricted access to the interdisciplinary curriculum to those students performing at or above grade level. This situation points to another constant of reform: Unintended consequences of any attempt at restructuring schoolwork will inevitably occur and need to be anticipated and addressed as they emerge.

CROSS-CASE ANALYSIS

As we noted at the start of this chapter, despite differences in these teachers' backgrounds, experience levels, and school settings, over the course of the reform their practices became more similar, their analysis of teaching and learning more sophisticated, and their learning opportunities more plentiful. Each of the schools in which they worked had become staffed by better-qualified teachers over the 3 years we studied them, and each school had improved student achievement on traditional test measures as well as in-house school assessments of reading that documented in more authentic ways books read and writing undertaken. The three case-study teachers are themselves well prepared and qualified: all are fully certified for the subjects they teach and have additional certification to work with English-language learners and gifted students. Their instruction provides better-than-adequate supports for student learning, featuring high expectations, a focus on standards, and demonstrated efforts to know their students not only as people but also as learners.

Commonalities in Practice and Philosophy

Strengthened by the reform were the abilities of each of the teachers to offer multiple avenues to reach students, provide varied materials to engage students with the content, and teach students learning strategies that cut across subject areas. As evidenced in the classrooms, each teacher found ways for students to take active roles in their own learning and reflect on their learning. All three teachers were organized and able planners, guided by standards and adept at "mapping backwards" from student learning goals. Each of them communicated with parents, participated in extracurricular activities, and sought professional-learning opportunities both within and beyond their school and the district. Each of them was working on creating a more student-centered learning environment—one more reflective of student needs—and providing more time for students to discuss and guide their own learning. And, like many of their peers, these teachers were attempting to exceed superficial implementation of the district's framework while integrating new ways of teaching into their repertoire.

Deeper and More Connected Learning Opportunities

As district and site professional development reflected the initial strong focus on literacy with workshops and study groups around such strategies as Read-Alouds, Guided Reading, and the Readers'/Writers' Workshop model, teachers both across the district and within schools developed a common language around the Literacy Framework. Though teachers were at different places with the framework—with respect to both acceptance and competence—the unified focus allowed teachers to work with one another within and across schools as they sought ways to incorporate, practice, and improve their own learning and teaching of literacy. Year by year, teachers were encouraged to develop their capacity to support literacy instruction. Thus, in the fall of 2001, when David Ruiz visited social studies teachers at Laurel Ridge who had incorporated literacy strategies into their teaching, he had already experienced school-level professional development on the Literacy Framework. The observations allowed him to see in practice what he had been thinking about and attempting in his own classroom.

Peer coach/staff developers influenced both the nature and frequency of professional development for all three teachers. Meeting each week as a group for district-led professional development and support, peer coach/staff developers played a role in building a "common language" throughout the district about instruction. As might be expected, the teachers had different access to their peer coaches, as well as different opinions about how effective they were. Ruiz had little one-on-one contact with peer coaches at Steward, mainly because the principal directed the peer coach to prioritize her time elsewhere and she assigned a consultant to work with social studies teachers. Murray had little praise for the peer coaches she encountered at Robinson, but she participated in professional development nonetheless, enthusiastic about adding more to her teaching repertoire. Ogden had positive rapport with her peer coaches and felt they supported her learning.

Each teacher experienced both large-group and small-group professional development, but spent more time in smaller collegial groups (e.g., learning groups, study groups) that met on a repeated basis than in larger ones convened for single-shot learning. This allowed the teachers to build relationships for longer-term inquiry and problem solving that could be connected to their students and the school and subject matter contexts in which they taught.

More Public Practice

David Ruiz, Leanne Murray, and Nancy Ogden all acknowledged that their work was becoming increasingly public. Over the course of 3 years, each of these teachers had opportunities to observe other teachers not only within their own department, grade level, and school, but also beyond their school and subject area. Principals, vice principals, peer coach/staff developers, other teachers, principal candidates, and instructional leaders had visited their classrooms—some for the brief walk-through visits, others for full-period observations. While Nancy Ogden noted that the burden of observers seemed to fall more heavily on language arts teachers, all teachers were observed more frequently in the third year of our research than in the first year. The typically isolated experience that Dan Lortie (1975) and others described as one of the regularities of schooling did not apply to these teachers.

Stronger Instructional Leadership

As part of the district-wide reform efforts, principals were required to identify a school-wide instructional focus each year from their observations and assessments of classroom teaching and learning. Ruiz's principal focused one year on "Shared Reading," one of the literacy strategies highlighted by the district, and the next year on "Purposeful Planning." Murray's principal emphasized a school-wide need to promote "Accountable Talk"[3] in classrooms; and Ogden's principal broadened her Accountable Talk focus from one year to a focus on "Student Engagement" the following year. The principals' roles as instructional leaders transformed the principals' work and influence on teaching. Principals were expected to evaluate teaching with greater scrutiny than before, determine where teachers needed to go next to develop their practice, motivate teachers to push themselves further, manage learning opportunities, and develop other supports as needed. In general, professional development and principals' instructional leadership aimed to promote a collaborative, reflective practice that supported teachers as they faced greater accountability for their teaching.

Increased Accountability

As we have mentioned, there were important conceptual distinctions between the high-stakes test-based accountability promoted by the state and the district's more instructionally oriented model of professional accountability. For our case-study teachers, however, the lines between state and district accountability blurred. In one ear, teachers heard the message from Anthony Alvarado, filtered through their principals, insisting that students would perform well on tests if they were taught well, and emphasizing a focus on teaching quality. In the other ear, teachers received messages directly from II/USP state-approved evaluators emphasizing a focus on the state test.

The teachers we followed were influenced by both messages. Nancy Ogden voiced the significant pressure she felt to help raise students' reading and writing scores. David Ruiz focused his attention more on the California High School Exit Exam (CAHSEE)—a test posing potentially more dire consequences for individual students than the SAT-9. And Leanne Murray, bemoaning the impact tests were having on student morale, preferred to rely on how students were progressing on specific standards. Despite their attention to (and concern about) high-stakes accountability measures, none of our case-study teachers implemented "drill and kill" test preparation. Rather, they reinforced reading strategies supported by the Literacy Framework and encouraged students to apply those strategies while taking tests.

All three teachers are in school environments where there is more professional and reciprocal accountability than there used to be. This is evidenced by more classroom observations, more direct instructional support from others, more teacher-to-teacher time devoted to matters of instruction, and the availability of more professional and classroom resources. Having more coherent and shared professional development seemed to have increased teachers' collective professional accountability. The presumption was that teachers knew the district's mission and vision, had been exposed to teaching strategies to support the vision, had had opportunities to observe them in practice, and had been encouraged to share their own struggles and successes with others. The range of strategies, and their triangulation, left little opportunity for teachers to claim they were unfamiliar with the district's teaching and learning goals.

Through formal and informal observations and evaluations, teachers experienced greater accountability for their teaching. Ruiz, as a new teacher, did not have much with which to compare current levels of observation other than his student-teaching experiences. However, although Ogden and Murray were accustomed to the presence of observers because they were showcased by their principals or supervised student teachers, those observations were less consequential to their instruction than observations now became. Ogden reflected the increased pressure she felt from a focused observation by the principal:

> I think it's just normal stress because there are so many factors that they're looking into, let's say, for Accountable Talk. There must be forty different guidelines they're looking for. And we're, of course, given the sheet, and this is what we're looking for in your classrooms, but am I covering everything? Did I miss anything? And you're trying to do your best job possible, but there's just so much that they're looking for. . . . I think all teachers feel the stress of having someone come in and formally observing them and looking for specifics. So it's a little bit intimidating. But at the same time I think it's good because they'll point out where our strengths are, where our weaknesses are.

All three teachers participated in peer observations in which they were encouraged to critique one another's practice in a constructive dialogue. The district hoped that as teachers experienced being observed and observing others more frequently and in focused ways, they would build the tools necessary to critique teaching more deeply.

Besides being accountable through observation, teachers were increasingly held accountable for using student data to inform instruction. While all teachers were encouraged to know their students as readers, language arts teachers carried the burden of this element of the accountability system. Language arts teachers at Steward, for example, met with the principal to review student scores and reading levels to begin a conversation about what students needed in their classrooms. No such requirement was levied on Ruiz. Ogden and Murray, on the other hand, met with their respective principals to review student gains on the San Diego reading tests from one year to the next. Ogden's principal also required a log of students' independent reading titles; this fostered meaningful conversations between her and language arts teachers about successes and challenges of particular students and classes.

Unintended Consequences

In addition to documenting many of the intended consequences of the districts' reforms, we came across a few unintended consequences.

These included significant changes in each teacher's student class composition, class size, and some frustrations with the reform.

Student Class Composition

As mentioned in chapter 6, a decrease in heterogeneity occurred in classrooms for most schools. Ogden and Murray, who for many years taught heterogeneous groups of students as defined by race, socioeconomic status, and achievement scores, experienced marked changes along these lines in their classroom compositions. Similarly, most of Ruiz's students were English-language learners who were more likely to be "clumped" together in his classes according to their two-hour or one-hour English class, which stratified students by language proficiency. Ogden's teaching was accessible to fewer lower-performing eighth-grade students since they were assigned to two-hour language arts classes that she did not teach. And students she used to share with another teacher by design were now shared only by chance. Murray had fewer heterogeneous groups of students since she was teaching GATE students for one period and low-performing sixth graders for three and a half hours a day.

There were many potential consequences of this stratification, including more focused and intensive instruction in reading and writing for students who were performing poorly on the district tests on the one hand, and more segregated classrooms with fewer models of high achievement and language proficiency for lower-achieving students on the other. Leaders may have initially made a strategic decision in establishing this trade-off, as teachers were learning new practices to address the needs of struggling students—research suggests that successful teaching of all children in widely heterogeneous classrooms requires greater skill and the ability to individualize instruction in sophisticated ways. It may be that a developmental approach to adult learning should focus first on the acquisition of new strategies and then to their application in more complex situations. Time will tell what the long-range outcomes of this decreased heterogeneity may prove to be and whether the district will adjust its strategies to seek to achieve more heterogeneity alongside more mature teaching strategies.

Class Size

The district reforms also impacted class size for all three teachers, in both predictable and unexpected ways. Data on class size for 1998, 2000, and 2001 reveal that average class sizes in social studies classes at all three schools increased by two to five students. In addition, as two-hour Literacy Block classes were kept below 25 students across the district, other language arts classes tended to expand. The average class size for language arts classes decreased overall at Steward by two students, most likely because such a high percentage of students required a Literacy Block class. However, the average class size increased at Laurel Ridge by two students, and at Robinson by four. This is in part due to the fact that in order to fund the "Blueprint," the district reduced the school discretionary funds that were used in previous years at Laurel Ridge and Robinson to lower class sizes across the board.

Frustrations with the Reform

Ruiz, Ogden, and Murray echoed some of the frustrations we heard from other teachers. The main complaint they shared was that teachers did not have substantial say as policies "came down from the top." While the district reform did not conflict with the three case-study teachers' ideas about instruction, it imposed threats to other aspects of teaching they held dear. Ruiz, a brand-new teacher desperate for more one-on-one support for his English-language learners, was particularly disappointed to lose classroom aides when the district cut funding for this position. Murray and Ogden feared the reform would undermine team structures deemed so valuable to their teaching. Said Ogden, "We are currently very frustrated with the district since their Literacy Blocks are threatening our teams and our ability to plan together to help students like we do with [our team]. . . . Basically we see that some of the reform efforts of the district are counter to the productive teaching we currently engage in." While Ogden's fears of losing her team did not play out, that fear was realized for Murray.

CONCLUSIONS

Taken together, these teachers' experiences illustrate the challenges and benefits of an intense, comprehensive systemic reform effort. While there have been fears, discomforts, and trade-offs, after the first 3 years of the reform each teacher had more coherent, deep professional-development opportunities available throughout the school year, and each had more knowledgeable and expert colleagues with whom to engage during their professional development. The teachers were all held accountable through multiple relationships to their students, peers, administration, other support providers, and the community. Teachers were encouraged to take risks in their teaching, to work and rework details in their instruction.

The extent to which each teacher's teaching changed depended substantially on each school's ability to build instructional capacity and the level of support each teacher took advantage of. As Rosenholtz (1991) suggests, teachers' conceptions of their work are influenced by interactions at the school, and the social organization of the workplace itself strongly affects their attitudes, cognitions, and behavior. Fulfilling the district's vision of powerful instruction required momumental work that needed to be enacted at the school level. Ensuring that schools emphasize powerful instruction as their core activity—and supporting them to develop meaningful, sustainable cycles of instructional improvement—depends upon principal leadership and prior history, as well as teacher expertise and collegial professional relationships. Those components, while improving at each of our case-study schools, still varied substantially for our case-study teachers.

The district appeared to be succeeding in enabling educators to acquire and share professional knowledge—for practice, in practice, and of practice (Cochran-Smith & Lytle, 1999). While each teacher faced challenges in developing a reflective practice, each was facing those challenges within a culture more equipped to prioritize student needs. The reform was clearly far from complete, and much work lay ahead, including the continual refinement of professional development to meet evolving teacher needs—and greater attention by the district to supportive school structures for teacher learning. If and when this is accomplished, perhaps

Cuban's metaphor for the impermeability of classroom practice to reform policies will no longer apply to San Diego City Schools.

NOTES

1. Prior to 2000–2001, eighth-grade students were required to submit a literacy portfolio, assessed centrally by teachers trained to do so during the summer. Ultimately this requirement was dropped, but Ruiz was trained in summer 2000.

2. Selection of a novel did not imply that teachers would necessarily teach that particular novel to the class in its entirety. In fact, the district's Literacy Framework encourages students to read books appropriate for their reading level. Some students might read the entire novel, but in many cases, the teacher selected portions of the book to demonstrate the use of a reading strategy that students would then apply to their own text.

3. Accountable Talk is a term that describes conversation that engages participants in active listening, requires participants to clarify or expand their ideas, present accurate information, substantiate their claims, and build on one another's ideas. Lucy Calkins (2001, p. 246) writes, "Children must be shown how to cultivate a climate of debate, questioning, and multiple interpretations. They must think about how to disagree with each other in ways that allow the other person to hear what is being said."

CHAPTER 8

Meeting the Needs of High Schools: Reforming the Reform

Although the elementary and middle schools made evident strides, San Diego's high school students remained the lowest-performing group in the district throughout the early years of the reform. While most of the district's students in grades 2–8 scored at or above the 50th percentile in reading by 2002, only 37% of students in grades 9–11 did so. (See Appendix). In addition to the very slow rate of improvement for high school students, the achievement gap was large, with only about 20% of African American and Latino high school students scoring at or above the norm in 1999, as compared to about 60% of White students. There was also a disjuncture between students' grades and their college readiness. Significant proportions of graduates from San Diego high schools with grade point averages of 3.2 and above still required remediation at the college level. Also of concern to the district was the dropout rate in high school, with noticeably fewer students at each successive grade level after ninth grade (SDCS, 2000).

All of these factors, plus the fact that the K–8 reform strategy clearly did not have adequate reach into high schools, ultimately propelled a revised system-wide effort at high school reform. To address the problem of low performance at the high school level, district leaders created new administrative structures and pursued grants to support focused work on high school reform. The stated mission of the effort was: "What the best and most exclusive schools do for their students, we will accomplish for all students" (SDCS, 2002a, p. 2). San Diego's attempt to reform its comprehensive high schools focused on three areas: reshaping principal leadership, increasing academic rigor within schools and classrooms, and creating personalized learning environments for students.

While Alvarado had brought a field-tested strategy for literacy reform in the lower grades, he did not seek to replicate the high school reform work done in New York, which relied on "birthing" new, small, instruction-focused schools where failing comprehensive high schools had once been (Darling-Hammond, Ancess, & Ort, 2001). San Diego constructed the challenge in a different way: how to change the culture of the comprehensive high school from stratified silos of private teacher practice to student- and instruction-focused institutions that would prepare all students to pursue college-level work.

As difficult as the initial reforms were in San Diego, these high aspirations for secondary school change promised to pose even greater conundrums. The push for high school reform from the central office raised another set of issues: specifically, how could a school district support instructional reform in its many diverse, comprehensive high schools? This chapter examines the district's ongoing efforts to learn to work with the high schools more effectively, as well as its efforts to stimulate more comprehensive high school reform.

HIGH SCHOOL IMPROVEMENT: NO MODEL TO FOLLOW

High schools have presented a perennial challenge to school reform efforts. In a study of system-wide K–12 reform efforts in Chicago, Sebring, Bryk, and Easton (1995) found consistent patterns of lower student achievement, lower engagement with reform and lower ratings of self-efficacy among teachers in high schools when compared to elementary schools. And while Chancellor of Instruction Anthony Alvarado's work in District No. 2 has been described as an "existence proof" that district-wide instructional improvement can happen (Elmore & Burney, 1999), it is important to note that District No. 2 serves a predominantly K–8 population with no large, comprehensive high schools under its jurisdiction.[1]

Widespread reform of high schools began as a more bottom-up process in New York City led largely by networks of reformers and philanthropists with the help of an Alternative Schools Division within the Board of Education (Darling-Hammond, 1997b). While the role of the district was crucial in the expansion of the small-schools movement in New York, the long-term history of small schools and the Alternative Schools Division of the New York City Board of Education for supporting such schools is unique. So unlike the field-tested reform approach for San Diego's elementary and middle schools, there were no directly analogous "working models" for instruction-focused, district-led, multischool reform at the high school level.

In addition to the lack of reform "models," comprehensive high schools are complex social institutions. Their large size, subject-based departmentalization, extensive extracurricular activities, internal stratification (tracking), and lack of instructional focus usually stymie reform efforts that attempt to target the teaching and learning core. Traditionally, high school principals have functioned more as operations managers than as leaders of instructional programs. Further, the notion of a neighborhood high school is deeply ingrained culturally; thus, efforts to change these schools encounter institutional pressures that typically reinforce the status quo.

Noting the challenges posed by the comprehensive high school, San Diego's reformers attempted to create in some deliberate ways a sense of urgency around the need for high school reform. Although high schools were already involved in the district-wide rollout of the Literacy and Math Frameworks, leaders recognized that more specific strategies needed to be tailored to high schools. To develop this agenda, the district successfully pursued planning grants from the Carnegie Corporation's Schools for a New Society program and from the U.S. Department of Education's Smaller Learning Communities initiative. Under the leadership of a high school reform planning team[2] and the newly hired high school reform coordinator, these grants were used to conduct research, gather stakeholder input and hold two principals' retreats. At the first of these retreats, the principals were presented with district-wide and school-specific student performance data, which leaders hoped would underscore the need for significant change at the high school level. In addition, the principals engaged in an action research project, where each one shadowed a student in his school for an entire day to catch a glimpse of the experience of attending their school from the perspective of a student. These shadowing experiences yielded some valuable insights as principals saw firsthand the lack of engagement and rigor in their classrooms.

It was also at this first retreat that district leaders introduced the three key areas for high school reform, intended to focus the work of the principals on what the high school reform group identified as most crucial: (1) increased academic press, achieved by reshaping instruction and course-taking patterns to challenge and motivate students; (2) improved instructional leadership among high school principals and greater distribution of leadership within high schools; and (3) the provision of more personalized educational settings for students. While these provided guiding principles for the high school reform initiative and were aligned with the district's overall strategy, more specific steps needed to be taken.

USING STATE POLICY AS A WARRANT
AND A TARGET FOR HIGH SCHOOL REFORM

Once again, Bersin and Alvarado used the external policy environment to leverage change. Across the nation, heightened graduation requirements and proficiency exams are becoming increasingly commonplace as states attempt to ratchet up the performance of their high school graduates. California has begun implementing a high school exit exam, which students must pass in order to receive a diploma, beginning in 2006. State content standards and related course requirements are approaching those of the university system. As in other areas of the reform, San Diego's leaders attempted to use these initiatives to serve their overall goals.

Starting with the first high school–specific reform retreat in February 2001, the district provided principals with disaggregated student performance data on a range of measures—standardized test scores, dropout rates, college eligibility and so on—in order to help principals see the patterns of chronic underperformance in their schools. Further, in an $8 million Carnegie Corporation Schools for a New Society grant, leaders of the high school reform initiative tethered local benchmarks for improvement to the University of California (UC) and California State University (CSU) subject area requirements. These course-taking requirements, often referred to as the "A–G's" because they specify expectations in seven content areas,[3] are the baseline requirements for admission to the state's public universities. The district pledged to increase the share of district graduates eligible for the UC/CSU system from the current 38% to 66% by 2004.

In its Carnegie Corporation grant, the district also set forth the expectation that by 2005, all students would pass the California High School Exit Exam (CAHSEE) by their senior year (SDCS, 2001). The district instituted a range of support programs for students not on target to pass the CAHSEE. Although reform leaders expected the number of underprepared students to decline sharply as the work of reform deepened at the K–8 level, at the start of a system-wide reform strategy, the remediation needs of high school students must be addressed. These needs, in combination with the district's response to California's call for the end of social promotion, undergirded the curricular reform strategies pursued in the early stage of San Diego's high school reform. Described further in the next section, these included Genre Studies courses for low-performing readers in 9th and 10th grades, overhaul of the mathematics curriculum and a strong set of supports for students to take and pass algebra (part of the state exit exam), and a new science curriculum.

This strategy was part of a general commitment to lead the reform from a curricular perspective. Unlike other attempts at high school reform, such as Philadelphia's, New York's and Boston's moves to create smaller learning communities (see, e.g., Darling-Hammond, 1997b; Fine, 1994; Raywid & Schmerler, 2003), San Diego reformers emphasized improving instruction rather than changing school structures. This emphasis was deliberate, as Alvarado and others believed that reculturing high schools was a necessary precursor to making structural changes that might support overall improvement. Alvarado endorsed the movement to create smaller learning communities, greater personalization, and longer blocks of learning time in the high schools, but he cautioned that "restructuring" was not the primary goal, but a means to an end:

> Structure cannot, does not, make reform happen. When you restructure a school, you cannot reform it. We have evidence of that in the literature. You actually have to re-culture a school and then you can actually get some reform. But, there are structural issues that get in the way of reform

because the improvement of instruction and the work that you need to do bumps up against these things that are there created by the system. So we need to start addressing those structures . . . But remember, this is Tony one-note, okay? [Laughter.] The one note is the improvement of instruction, leading instructional improvement. This should not be interpreted as changing that basic theme. [Structure] is something to look at that we can change to enhance the ability to actually [lead instructional improvement].

CHANGING CURRICULUM AND INSTRUCTION: THE ENGINE OF THE REFORM

Literacy Reform at the High School Level

From early on, the district-wide literacy initiative had its own elements at the high school level. In addition to the introduction of peer coach/staff developers and the rollout of the Literacy Framework, the "Blueprint" specified Genre Studies classes in the 9th and 10th grades for students below grade level in reading as assessed by Stanford Diagnostic Reading Test (SDRT) and Individual Reading Inventory (IRI) scores. Later known as the two-hour Literacy Block, these courses were intended to support students in the development of reading skills across a variety of genres. An even more intensive version, the three-hour Literacy Core, was designed for ninth-grade students who fell significantly below grade level. Members of the district's literacy department and a team of consultants trained teachers of these courses in the elements of the district's Literacy Framework as well as the workshop model of instruction in reading and writing. The "Blueprint" allocated funds to these teachers to establish classroom libraries to entice struggling readers, and teachers were expected to create classroom environments that supported student learning by employing student- and teacher-created informational charts and posting models of exemplary student work.

This approach to literacy reform at the high school level clashed with some deep-seated beliefs about English classrooms. First, the focus on genre, with a heavy emphasis on nonfiction texts, challenged the primacy of the canon in English classrooms. Teachers were also expected to help students find books at their reading level; this demand conflicted with the tradition of teaching one work to an entire class. Moreover, as most high school English teachers are literature majors, few if any arrive at the high school prepared to teach struggling students how to read. As a member of the district's literacy department observed:

> High school teachers, including the peer coach/staff developers, don't have a lot of knowledge about the teaching of reading. They became English teachers because they love literature, and they're now faced with the reality that they have kids sitting in front of them who are reading at the third, fourth, fifth, or sixth grade level and can't tackle that literature.

In addition, many new teachers were assigned to teach the Literacy Block and Core classes, augmenting the already immense need for professional development with demands for support in such areas as classroom management. Many teachers also viewed the courses as a detrimental form of tracking, as the students were homogeneously grouped by performance level. Furthermore, since the multiperiod class constrained their schedule, many block and core students traveled together to all of their classes, reinforcing the segregative effects of grouping.

While some teachers enjoyed this new approach to teaching their subject matter, the contentiousness surrounding the district's reforms made them reluctant to share their successes. As a literacy consultant to the district observed: "There are a lot of people who are excited, after they've tried some of these things, and that's great. But the sad thing is, some of them feel they have to hide in their classrooms because the people who are resistant are so outspoken, and the teachers who are on board don't want to be seen as stooges for the administration." As a focus area of the "Blueprint," the teachers of the Literacy Core and Block classes were also far more likely than their peers in higher-grade or higher-level courses to be visited by the principal and district staff during walk-throughs.

The success record of the literacy reforms at the high school level was mixed. Some early SDRT data for ninth graders suggested that students in the two-hour course were making above-expected gains (SDCS, 2002a). However, in the face of budget cuts in 2002–2003, the three-hour Literacy Core class was eliminated. Few lamented this change given that the course had failed to produce the hoped-for multiyear gains, but some observers noted that the potential of the class was never realized. The initial design would have placed reading specialists in the three-hour block classes to support teachers' efforts in building literacy skills among their students. Further, with so many of the core teachers new not only to the profession but also the district's framework and the workshop model, the professional-development demands taxed a literacy department that focused its resources on the lower grades. District leaders within and outside of the literacy department hoped that the role of content administrator in literacy, with peer coach/staff developers still in place at lower-performing sites, could offer on-site, context-specific professional development to English teachers, but the positions were difficult to fill.

Although high school reading scores showed little immediate improvement, the Literacy Framework and adoption of the workshop model created a common language for conversations about literacy, which supported later changes in practice. As a member of the literacy department asserted:

> The conversation among the high school principals has changed dramatically from when I first started doing this until now. They sustain a conversation about literacy instruction and the challenges they're facing at their school, whereas, in year 1, it wasn't like that, I'm telling you.

The disciplinary norms confronted by this approach to literacy reform should not be understated, as the district's strategies called into serious question both curricular and pedagogical traditions. If norms around English teaching are in fact changing—particularly, shifting from liter*ature* to liter*acy*—they are likely to do so slowly (Siskin & Little, 1995). While much work remained for literacy reforms to yield substantial improvement at the high school level, there was also a question of resources. As a member of the literacy department observed, "I don't think that we have changed enough to impact student achievement yet at high school. But I think also that high schools need a lot more support in this effort than they currently have."

Math Reforms

Mathematics was also on the radar screen since the early days of the reform; the district's math department introduced a mathematics framework with the second-year "Blueprint" in 2001. Bridging state and district standards and influenced by the national Curriculum and Evaluation Standards for School Mathematics (NCTM, 1989), the district's Math Framework focuses on two categories: mathematical content (four strands of mathematics, including number sense and operations; functions and algebra; measurement and geometry; and data analysis, statistics and probability, and mathematical processes) and mathematical processes (the tools and habits of mind used when solving problems). The math processes consist of "quantitative literacy, computational fluency, problem solving, use of representations, use of reason and proof, ways to communicate about math, and the ability to make connections" (SDCS, 2003a).

As with the literacy reforms, the math reforms at the high school level focused on the most vulnerable students: ninth graders who were performing below grade level and who had not successfully completed algebra. Based on their performance on a geometry readiness test, low-performing students were placed in a new course entitled Algebra Explorations. At most high schools, this was a single-period course, but a small number of high schools elected to offer two-period intensive support classes for these students.

The philosophy behind the Algebra Explorations class was to strengthen students' skills in algebraic functions and for students to learn mathematics concepts through solving "real world" problems using an inquiry approach. A new textbook, *Discovering Algebra*, and graphing calculators were also adopted as part of the new curriculum. Teachers were offered professional development during the summer months to prepare to teach the new course and integrate technology into their instruction, and were provided ongoing sessions during the academic year.

Just as the literacy strategies confronted old, well-ensconced norms, so the conceptual approach to mathematics embedded in these new curricular materials challenged the focus on computation that had driven much of the math curriculum, particularly at the high school level. The district math director acknowledged mistakes made with the introduction of Algebra Explorations, including the provision of worksheets to teachers to help them access the curriculum; these worksheets inadvertently oversimplified the intended approach. Still, the district math director found that the problems with implementing the new curriculum—and with integrating technology—went well beyond the way it was introduced. In contrast to the inroads being made in elementary and middle school mathematics, the director exclaimed:

> [I]n terms of high school reform . . . there's so much to do. It's incredible! It's incredible! I go to classrooms and I come back reeling with . . . what part of what we've been trying to teach have we not been teaching well enough that they get it? . . . How do they think what they're doing is okay? So we've got to get smarter about this whole thing.

While some math departments embraced standards mapping as an approach to curricular reform, the math director cautioned that this could also be a trap. As she explained, "They're simplifying the task at the cost of improving the learning by saying that, 'if I do standards alignment, I'm going to get some results.' 'Okay, let's pick our standards that we're not teaching very well and let's teach these really hard right now,' and they take them out of context and they teach them in a procedural way with the ideas not connected to other ideas and concepts, and I don't think that's going to be very likely to help kids move forward."

Math reforms at the high school level have barely scratched the surface, but the math director nonetheless hopes that if math administrators can be mobilized in effective ways, they may be able to move departmental practice and student achievement forward:

> I think [the role of math administrator] has incredible potential. You've got to choose the right people and you've got to give them the right training and they have to be in a context that supports them. So if I can have all those things in place, then I think it's great. And I think it has incredible potential because it's making public the practice of teaching at the high school which hasn't been public before.

However, in the very early stages of that role, these math administrators needed support to develop their leadership skills but they were not always employed at school sites in ways that supported teaching and learning in mathematics. The district math department continued to try to support these growing leaders and created on-site professional development opportunities for Algebra Explorations teachers whether or not the schools had math administrators. But as this exchange from a group of high school math teachers during an on-site Algebra Explorations professional-development day suggests, the math director was not far off base when she said that "the high school is the hardest thing to change":

TEACHER 1: I have some kids who would get it wrong today, right in a week, and wrong a week after that. They don't work for quality. They work to get it done.

TEACHER 2: If we do less and work harder with less, maybe they'll do better.

TEACHER 1: Our kids aren't going to try hard, that's why they're at where they're at.

TEACHER 3: I have GATE [Gifted and Talented Education] kids in [Algebra Explorations]—how do they get into this class?

TEACHER 1: Drill and practice, drill and practice. That will help our students.

TEACHER 2: If they do it.

After several years of effort, much work remained, particularly in developing pedagogy to teach math content and developing norms about students' capacities to learn. During the 2002–2003 school year, half of the monthly principals' conferences were dedicated to math in order to orient principals to issues of math reform and to develop their leadership to support changes in curriculum and instruction in their mathematics classrooms. And guided by the district's math leadership, providers of mathematics professional development endeavored to provide principals and teachers with concept-based and curriculum-embedded learning experiences as they modeled the type of teaching they wished to see in math classrooms (see Stein, Smith, & Silver, 1999). Progress was being made, and achievement was inching upward, but there was clearly a great deal of work to be done. Perhaps most promising, there was finally a growing consensus that this work, and a pathway to follow in accomplishing it, was needed.

Science Reforms at the High School Level

Unlike the literacy and math approaches, which were initially rooted in the earlier grades and moved up to the high school, the district's science department was charged with beginning its curricular reform at the high school level and moving down. The change in course of study in science provides another example of the district's "active use" of state policy (Firestone, 1989). Citing the state's content standards, which require more than the previously required 2 years of high school science, the district increased the local requirement to 3 years of laboratory science for all high school students. This move aligned district policy with both state standards and university entrance requirements, yet also presented the district with the puzzle of how to provide rigorous laboratory science to all of its students, regardless of performance level. To address this challenge, the district reordered its sequence of science courses—a change long advocated by leaders in science instruction—and adopted a curriculum developed by the American Association of Physics Teachers called "Active Physics" to be used with all ninth-grade students. Although contentious, this change advanced the district's agenda of providing access to improved pedagogy, as Active Physics incorporated the type of learner-centered, inquiry-based approach advocated by the district. It also served the district's equity goals by increasing access to challenging, college-preparatory content across the system of high schools.

Although the district engaged science teachers in discussions prior to making the change, not everyone perceived this inclusion. As one principal described:

> Another example [of the speed of reform implementation in San Diego] is two weeks ago we changed the science instruction and curriculum in San Diego City Schools. The change came as a surprise to everyone. Not one science teacher knew that a discussion was on about how science was implemented in San Diego City Schools. They didn't even know there was a discussion, let alone there was going to be a change. And one day it's the way it's always been for the last 50 years, and the next day they said, "Okay, we're going to reverse this. The 9th grade is going to do this, the 10th graders are going to do this. This class is out. Change this name." And it just caught us off-guard. It feels as if there's a disconnect between the practitioners at the sites and the district leadership.

The district science director acknowledged the difficult situation created by the physics adoption, which many considered to be top down, but defended the decision:

> [The traditional text] is not an inquiry-based curriculum. It was developed before the National Science Education standards even existed. So, we would have then been trying not only to have ninth grade physics implemented but to turn a curriculum that isn't something into something that we think is what we are about. It wouldn't have worked. Would it have been easier? Oh, yeah, but it wouldn't have brought about the needed reform.

The department was far more transparent in its approach to chemistry and biology reforms, working with teacher volunteers to field-test new curriculum and giving participants structured opportunities to provide feedback to help prepare for district-wide rollout.

As with the other content areas, the science department paid explicit attention to the pedagogy used with adult learners in on- and off-site professional-development opportunities. For example, as it launched a new approach to textbook selection, it discovered the need to offer professional development in the practice of inquiry as well as in the specific curriculum. As the science director commented:

> [The physics teachers] loved the fact that they were getting adult-level content in a summer institute that directly connected to the student curriculum as well as the pedagogy that was all a part of it, so it was like the evaluations said, "Thank you for not wasting my time. I've gone to so many of these workshops where I can't use what I'm getting. This is directly applicable to my kids and my classroom. I have the strategies I need. I understand how the curriculum works." It was that kind of feedback.

Since the physics program addressed the whole ninth grade and not just the lowest performers, the introduction of the new curriculum unearthed a different kind of resistance among principals, teachers, parents and community members. In essence, the fact that the science reforms substantially "detracked" science courses[4] was one source of concern voiced by some teachers as well as some affluent parents who did not want to disturb the more stratified system that they felt had served their children well. Indeed, it was at the same school board meeting where the science department brought the physics reform proposal forward that La Jolla High School, a high-scoring school located in a high-wealth area of the district, proposed charter status to gain autonomy from the "Blueprint" and other district curricular mandates, particularly the sweeping changes in science. (The district later worked out an arrangement offering some autonomy to La Jolla in order to keep it in the district).

As the science department moved forward with new curriculum in chemistry and biology, it learned from its experiences with physics. Most important to sustain, the science director asserted, was the professional learning community established among science teachers within each discipline as they learn skills of inquiry and experience new curricula: "[O]ne of the things that has come back loud and clear, and I think has helped set the stage for chemistry, is they really value the time to have a professional learning community, and they really see themselves as a community of physics teachers." The science department was still struggling with how to support teachers to use professional development time effectively and how to utilize science administrators in ways that would impact student achievement. The extent to which these efforts in science result in greater learning, particularly vis-à-vis standards-based tests, remains to be seen, but the approach to professional development around inquiry, content and a specific curriculum reflects a growing consensus in education research about the types of adult-learning experiences that are likely to yield changes in teaching practice (Cohen & Hill, 2000; Putnam & Borko, 2000; Wilson & Berne, 1999).

ORGANIZATIONAL STRATEGIES

The initially limited success of the curricular interventions described above encouraged district leaders, over time, to seek to adjust the system-wide reform approach to better meet the needs of high schools. Indeed, while the district's reform theory focused on the instructional core as the locus of change, San Diego's experiences with high school indicated that, in addition to well-grounded theories of learning and change, leaders also needed to develop a theory of the organization, particularly when dealing with schools of the size and organizational complexity of the comprehensive high school.

Creating High School Communities of Learning

As we have noted, a frequent criticism of school reform in San Diego under Bersin and Alvarado was its top-down nature. As Hightower (2001) observes, San Diego's reform strategy created a tension between the "what" and the "how" of reform, with teachers and principals generally admitting value in the content of the changes effected by district leaders, but finding the way they were introduced unsettling. At the high school level, however, principals and teachers were more likely to question both the "what" and the "how," raising concerns about the appropriateness of district strategies for high school improvement.

The district's earlier system-wide strategy with little differentiation by grade level created Learning Communities, clusters of schools that were heterogeneously grouped by geography and school level, as the venue for professional development and collaboration. While Alvarado recognized the potential value of grade-level groupings, he feared that creating such groups would minimize "the K–12 thinking that has to go on" (Hightower, 2001, p. 137). Increasingly, however, high school principals bristled at the lack of attention to what they saw as "their" issues. They were concerned about the level of knowledge reformers had about the particular needs of high schools and felt that K–12 instructional conferences were not supplying them with the tools necessary to do their job. In 2000, large majorities of high school principals responding to a survey felt that the work that went on in the Learning Communities was not helpful to them, and the district did not understand their school's reform agenda.

District leaders increasingly recognized this disconnect, and began crafting a reform approach that was more specific to high school. One of the first organizational responses to the high school reform question was the creation of more homogeneous learning communities. With the departure of an instructional leader, district reformers had an opportunity to redesign the groupings. They paired one instructional leader with extensive high school experience with a new candidate with a background in middle school, high school, and special education to create two high school–only Learning Communities. Following approval from the school board for this action, Bersin commented on the change at a K–12 principals' conference:

> [H]igh schools, in fact, require not separate treatment but different treatment. There is [grade-level] difference, and we have to take it into account. . . . Without cutting ourselves adrift from our colleagues and understanding that what happens in the elementary school is absolutely critical to the success of our students in high school, we also will confront the fact that high schools require their own approaches to reform. (Hightower, 2001, p. 248)

The high school Learning Communities, under the two original instructional leaders, endured for 3 years. During that time, the three guiding principles of personalization, academic rigor, and instructional leadership remained the focus of high school reform.

In addition to creating the two new Learning Communities, district leaders began to collaborate more with the high school principals on the work of school improvement. Increasingly, district administrators have turned to the schools themselves—and the expertise that exists within them—for more guidance and direction as the high school reform initiative continues to unfold. For example, at a high school principals' conference at the end of 2001, Alvarado asked a group of principals to conduct research and prepare recommendations regarding changes in daily schedules and school-year calendars that might better support instruction. The principals seemed willing to do the work, but also skeptical that district leaders would heed their input. Alvarado reiterated the position that neither he nor other district administrators had an answer in mind and that the request for input was genuine. One of the principals attempted to express the sentiment of the group, noting that being viewed as resources to inform change would, for them, present a departure from the district practice to which they had grown accustomed:

> So now to have us engaged in this kind of discussion to, if we go forward, understanding that there's got to be some fundamental trust and that you're reaching out and you're trying to work with folks as opposed to "you are going to do it or else" . . . that's when people will want to work harmoniously together, because then that would be great and might

help you out quite a bit, because there is some intelligence in this room that's pretty doggone good. . . . So I applaud you for allowing this dialogue to occur. And hopefully we'll continue to have it so we can continue to feel that we are in this thing together.

Subsequently, a regrouping of the high schools into "study groups" designed around common reform issues constituted another step toward engaging high school principals in the development of context-relevant reform approaches. Begun with a charge from the superintendent to differentiate supports to the high schools based on local needs, the high school instructional leaders, along with their colleagues, devised study groups, subsets of high schools organized around "academic performance and other needs identified by each school's stakeholder groups" (SDCS, 2003b). The groupings included the "challenge" schools, higher-performing schools with a need to address persistent achievement gaps among groups of students; "community engagement" schools, charged with improving student achievement to retain resident students who might opt to attend other high schools while also involving families of students who travel from other parts of the city to the schools; "redesign" schools, which were charged with securing to open as complexes of small schools, some as early as 2004; and the district's extant alternative schools. In addition, San Diego City Schools began exploring opportunities for the development of new small high schools, securing funding from the Bill and Melinda Gates Foundation to support the work of the redesign schools as well as the development of new small high schools.

While principals experienced their study groups differently, the evidence suggests that they appreciated the district's attempt to better tailor resources and supports to their site needs. In particular, the challenge schools anticipated the possibility of greater autonomy if they showed continued improvements in student achievement and narrowed the achievement gap. The redesign principals capitalized on opportunities to work together and learn from one another as they ventured into uncharted waters of comprehensive high school restructuring. As one of the redesign principals reflected:

We talk about the importance of collaboration for our teachers and how motivating it is, and we talk about the need for differentiated staff development—well, this is the truest form of differentiated staff development, these groupings based on need and similar objectives. Even though all of our schools are unique in many respects, we are grouped with very like objectives in mind. And you do learn so much from each other, and you're not reinventing the wheel alone.

Since the study groups were designed to be flexible to school needs, district leaders will likely continue to adapt the groups and the strategies as needs and performance levels continue to change. However, the guiding principles of the district's high school reform—leadership, personalization, and rigor—have shaped and continue to shape the work of these groups.

Focusing on Leadership, Personalization, Rigor

Leadership

District leaders have endeavored to shift the focus of the high school principalship from operations management toward instructional leadership, a normative shift at least as great as, if not greater than, the norm changes embodied in the curricular reforms described above. Doing so has involved including principals in instruction-focused professional development; for example, guiding principals through activities modeled after readers' workshop approaches or inquiry-based mathematics lessons to help them understand what to look for in classrooms. Additionally, instructional leaders have pushed principals to increase the amount of time they spend in their teachers' classrooms, and to do so beyond the formal evaluation role in order to develop a sense of the level of teaching quality in their schools and to identify common professional-development needs. Instructional leaders have urged high school principals to spend the equivalent of 3 days per week in classrooms, which for many entails a reversal in the typical balance of a high school principal's time allocation from operational issues to instructional ones.

As in the lower grades, district leaders used the walk-through in high schools as a tool to assess teaching quality. As Elaine Fink (a former superintendent of New York's District No. 2 whom Alvarado brought to San Diego to work with principals and instructional leaders) described at the initial high school principals' retreat in February

2001, "On walk-throughs, we'll be looking at basically three things: (1) the level of teaching practice, (2) student engagement with the teaching practice, and (3) how the classroom supports learning." At this same retreat, Fink emphasized that principals should not let their lack of knowledge in every content area impede them from assessing instructional quality in their school:

> [T]his is not about being a content specialist—there is no way you can be specialists in all the content areas. . . . It's about distinguishing good instruction from poor instruction. And then figuring out how I get poor instruction to become excellent instruction.

While research examining connections between leadership and learning suggests that content knowledge does indeed matter for leadership (e.g., Stein & D'Amico, 2000), and the district endeavored to increase principals' content-specific knowledge through professional development, it was central to the district's notion of principal instructional leadership that school leaders develop an eye for instructional quality across content areas.

To respond to the demands of subject-based departmentalization, the district established new roles to support three core subject areas by creating the position of content administrators in literacy, math and science. Some math and literacy administrators were placed at sites in 2001–2002; additional administrators, including those in science, were initially placed in 2002–2003. These vice principal-level positions were intended to provide on-site, discipline-specific support to teachers and discipline-specific analyses of teaching. Ideally, these individuals spent their time in classrooms, working side-by-side with teachers observing, coaching and modeling lessons, and planning professional development based on local needs. District leaders in the core content areas commented that certain individuals in these roles made strides at their high schools. At the same time, the initial implementation of the role met challenges. Some district staff questioned how content administrators were being used at sites, particularly the appropriateness of their use for activity supervision and test administration. At the same time, principals claimed that they were unclear on exactly what these individuals were permitted to do and felt they should share in the high school's administrative burden.

While some content administrators were standouts in their new roles, both principals and district staff learned that it is difficult to locate individuals with strengths in both leadership *and* content, the two skill areas emerging as crucial to success in the role. Given the evaluation component of the content administrator position, many qualified teachers chose not to pursue the role so as to not change their status vis-à-vis their peers. And in the case of English, where the role of peer coach/staff developer was already in place, many of those individuals applied for and were promoted to literacy administrator positions, creating a number of peer coach vacancies that remained empty for some time. Last, the degree of support across departments varied: while the math and science administrators met weekly with their district supervisors for professional development and support during 2002–2003, the limited resources in secondary literacy allowed far less frequent opportunities for high school literacy administrators to learn from one another.

Although content administrators gave principals "extra sets of eyes" to monitor and support classroom practice in the core areas, district content leaders emphasized that principals still play an important role in shaping the opportunities available to these new leaders. With content administrators in place, principals should not assume that math or literacy is "off their plate"; instead, district leaders urged principals to consider how they could support these individuals to move their school's efforts forward in each subject area, and how they could stay aware of what the content administrators were doing to make sure it was appropriate to their role.

Academic Rigor

District leaders recognized that increasing the rigor in San Diego's high school classrooms would require a coordinated, multifaceted approach with the ongoing provision of pressure and support. In addition to offering professional-development opportunities to teachers and principals, district leaders directed principals and counselors to closely examine course offerings in an effort to direct more of the high school curriculum toward college preparatory courses. Additionally, district content area leaders worked with teachers to develop standards-aligned end-of-course assessments to bring commonality and focus to how core courses are taught. The district also directed schools to enhance extended-learning opportunities, both during and after school and in the summer, to support students who were falling behind in district graduation requirements. With all of these efforts underway, by 2002–2003, there was a sense of progress among many at the high school level. As one instructional leader noted:

> The changes I have noticed at the high school that are positive are: teachers becoming less resistant, many teachers really wanting to figure it out and adjust not only for the implementation issues but looking at needs of students, and not just teaching the course or the curriculum or the book, but really trying to adjust to the needs of students. The [other] major change I've seen at the high school level is that I don't think there's any doubt in anyone's mind that the major responsibility [principals] are being held accountable for is to lead the improvement of instruction.

Personalization

Even as curriculum and instruction were strengthened, concerns about personalization arose from the repeated finding that high school students, particularly in large schools, do not feel connected to their schools or known by their teachers (e.g., Powell, Farrar, & Cohen, 1985). District leaders hoped that by creating opportunities for connectedness through peer mentoring, smaller class sizes, and longer blocks of learning time, students would be more engaged in school experiences and their learning. However, these incremental changes do not fundamentally change the key instructional and relational problems of high school education. At the root, it is difficult if not impossible to get high school teachers to focus on the individual learning needs of pupils if they see more than 100 students a day in the factory-model schedule that was inherited from reforms of nearly a century ago. Without a major restructuring of how the high school operates, serious instructional reform may be a pipe dream.

Consequently, San Diego finally decided to move forward with the redesign of a subset of its large comprehensive high schools into small, autonomous schools and to examine opportunities to create new small schools. During the 2003–2004 school year, three chronically low-performing SDCS high schools began intensive research, planning, and community engagement toward transforming their campuses into complexes of small, autonomous schools. Using *Redesigning Schools: What Matters and What Works* (Darling-Hammond, 2002) as a framework, and garnering significant support from the district's School-to-Career office, the schools held retreats, participated in study tours and institutes, and received majority votes of their staffs in favor of moving forward with redesign.

The three schools in this first cohort were all ethnically and linguistically diverse, serving high proportions of students eligible for free or reduced-price lunch, and struggling to meet state and district accountability targets. The principals and staffs at the schools were committed to creating more personalized school environments where teachers could know their students as individual learners, where teachers knew one another and could collaborate on issues of subject matter and student needs, and where teachers could feel a sense of ownership over school policies and practices. At each site, design teams developed plans for the new autonomous schools to send to the Board of Education. On November 25, 2003, the Bill and Melinda Gates Foundation announced an $11 million grant to SDCS to support the work of this first cohort of redesign high schools. Given the context of SDCS's high school reform efforts to this point, the explicit treatment of structure as a barrier to school improvement represented an important change in direction in the district, one that was closely watched as the results at these redesign schools were expected to inform future attempts to harness structures for instructional purposes.

Collaboration in Reform: A Changing Landscape

Together, these changes in the ways the district worked with high schools as a group and conceived of the role of school structure in improving outcomes—perhaps constituting an emerging theory of organization—appeared to advance the high school reform agenda. According to CTP survey data, by 2003 high school principals perceived that the district was learning to work with them more effectively, and that they benefited from the opportunity to work with their high school colleagues in the regrouped Learning Communities. Whereas only 25% of high school principals found discussions in their Learning Communities helpful to them in 2000 (when they were in heterogeneous groups with elementary and middle school principals), in 2003, 85% of them found these discussions valuable. By 2003, more principals—now a solid majority—found monthly principals' conferences useful, and few now felt that the district failed to understand their school's reform efforts (see Table 8.1).

Furthermore, the survey data indicated that, as compared to 2000, by 2003 principals felt district priorities were more aligned with their school priorities; they felt more in synch with district beliefs and norms about practice and more comfortable speaking up at district meetings (see Table 8.2).

Changes in Reform Technology: Developing an "Ambidextrous" School District

The need for adjustments to the high school reform agenda reveals an interesting phenomenon in the technology of reform. As we have discussed, the district's initial approach seemed to have had the most traction in the elementary schools (see chapter 5), and made strong headway in the middle schools (see chapter 6). This finding may be due to the fact that the reform technology was better suited to the lower grades, where it had been piloted. Elementary schools are typically

Table 8.1. Principal Survey Results Regarding District Reforms

Survey Item	High School Principals (2000) N= 12	High School Principals (2003) N= 13
The district does *not* understand my school's reform agenda (*percent rating "agree" or "strongly agree"*)	41%	23%
Please rate how valuable monthly principals' conferences have been to you and your work (*percent rating item "highly valuable"*)	50%	62%
Please rate how valuable discussions with principals in your Learning Community have been to you and your work (*percent rating item "highly valuable"*)	25%	85%

Source: CTP Principal Survey, May 2000 and May 2003. In 2000, principals were surveyed district-wide; in 2003, only high school principals were surveyed by CTP. The high school sample excludes atypical and pilot schools.

Table 8.2.   San Diego High School Principal Views of District Norms and Priorities

Responses to: "Please indicate how strongly you agree or disagree with the following statements regarding your district" (1 = strongly disagree and 5 = strongly agree)	Mean (2000) N = 12	Mean (2003) N = 13
District priorities are consistent with my school's priorities	3.7	4.2
I am comfortable asking questions or speaking up during district meetings	3.5	4.1
In this district, we hold common beliefs and norms of practice	3.2	4.0

Source: CTP Principal Survey, May 2000 and May 2003. The high school sample excludes atypical and pilot schools.

smaller and less structurally complex than their secondary counterparts. They are also more focused on the development of the "gateway" skills of literacy and math, upon which the reform concentrated. The strategy for change had been well worked out in other elementary school contexts, so it was possible—though not easy—to implement a reasonably well-formed approach in a relatively standardized way throughout the district and achieve strong results.

On the other hand, high schools were both less suited to the content of the initial reform and less structurally responsive to its strategies. Furthermore, efforts to redesign urban high schools nationally suggest there is not a well-defined technology for successful high school education in many cities, nor a particularly well-developed set of strategies for changing these institutions. The evolution of more high school–specific strategies, particularly as they engage issues of organizational structure by fostering innovation from the "bottom up," may represent an instance of the district becoming a more "ambidextrous" organization (Tushman & O'Reilly, 1996). Such organizations may pursue quality in a well-developed part of their operation by aggressively pursuing a strategy that has been tested and found productive. At the same time, in another area where knowledge is less certain and the technology is less clear, the same organization may seek to foster experimentation in order to find out what works before it invests in new forms of production. With one hand, the organization manages a tightly coupled approach to quality development, while with the other it manages a process of innovation for another aspect of the enterprise.

Similarly, while pursuing with one hand a set of well-configured strategies to continue to achieve incremental improvements in the literacy and math reforms in the lower grades, district leaders began working with high school principals to encourage innovation, particularly in the development of new organizational structures, with the other. Perhaps, as a study of successful business firms suggests, the district can strengthen its core technology of teaching and learning by focusing on polishing its reform at the lower grades while encouraging "variation, selection, and retention" (Tushman & O'Reilly, 1996, p. 27) with respect to novel high school reform strategies that appear promising.

OUTLOOK FOR HIGH SCHOOL REFORM

While high school performance data remained, by and large, frustratingly low at the high school level, it began to turn around. For example, one study of the "Blueprint" outcomes found declines in reading/literacy and mathematics scores for San Diego's high school students from 2000–2002 relative to other schools in the state. However, in 2002–2003, a much higher percentage of San Diego's high schools met both state school-wide and subgroup targets (56%, or 9 of 16, versus 19%, or 3 of 16, in 2001–2002) (Quick et al., 2003, p. 91). In addition, the reform made inroads with principals that could well be important precursors to the changes in instruction the district hopes will raise student achievement. As one of the instructional leaders reflected:

> I would say, if anyone asks what I see as the improvement, number one, it's the culture change that has occurred amongst the high school principals. Having been there, I know that it was a culture focused on operational issues, on maintaining a calm, safe environment in the school. I think we knew we should be in classrooms, but the reality of that was not happening. So the culture of changing the focus of the principal on being the instructional leader has definitely occurred. . . . [O]bviously, we have a long way to go, but I think that should be seen as a very significant change.

Building on a sustained, multiyear focus on improving instruction, particularly in courses serving the lowest-performing students, and heading the district-led push to reculture the high school principalship into an instructional leadership position, San Diego City Schools positioned itself to begin to make the real improvements in secondary student performance that had thus far eluded them.

As one of the high school instructional leaders commented, thinking back on his work since the first high school reform retreat:

> [T]his is really only 2 years at high school that this focus has been on doing something different. That's not a long time, and I would suspect it takes at least 5 years to see something change in your product, but we can't waste that much time. So, the urgency's got to be kept on, somebody's got to keep pushing these people, you've got to think through the supports, and you've got to build them up when they don't think they're making it.

With the retirement of the two original high school instructional leaders in July 2003, the district hoped it had found that continued push in its new high school administrator, a former high school principal in San Diego County with a track record of improving achievement outcomes and access to college for diverse student populations. With this new role in place, foundation funds to support school redesign, and a renewed focus on high school reform led by the superintendent, there was a chance that high school reform in San Diego would not fade soon. What remained to be seen was whether the changes that had been made thus far were indeed the antecedent steps that establish the foundation from which student achievement can appreciably improve, and whether the first cohort of redesigned high schools would in time demonstrate the efficacy of combining a structural approach with the instructional reforms already in place.

NOTES

1. In New York City, the comprehensive high schools as a group have historically constituted their own separate district, the "High School District." However, Alvarado sponsored a number of small high schools of choice in both District Nos. 2 and 4 when he was superintendent.

2. This team included district directors of core content areas, guidance, extended learning, standards and accountability, and school-to-career, two instructional leaders, and four high school principals.

3. The seven areas are social science, English, mathematics, laboratory science, languages other than English, visual and performing arts, and college-preparatory electives.

4. An honors Active Physics course, an augmented version of the "regular" curriculum, was developed, but it still differed from the traditional honors or AP physics course offered previously in the district.

CHAPTER 9

Conclusion

When looked at from both "inside-out" and "outside-in" perspectives, the San Diego reform provides a fascinating case of a systemic reform initiative that prioritized high-quality instruction and professional learning. It did so through a forceful district-led agenda that turned many traditional notions of the relationship between bureaucracy and innovation upside down. It sought to empower teachers and principals at the "bottom" of the system to solve problems more effectively by organizing intensive professional-development opportunities that would enhance their expertise and by creating a culture of shared norms of practice from the "top" and "bottom" simultaneously. At the same time, the district attempted to change the culture of a large organization and move it quickly in a common direction with strong interventions from the top of the system that affected every aspect of operations throughout the enterprise, ranging from organizational structures and budget allocations to hiring, evaluation, and retention of personnel to curriculum and instruction—the core technology of education. This created the paradoxical situation in which those being empowered with greater knowledge felt less empowered and autonomous in making many decisions, especially during the first 3 years of the reform. It also engendered the inevitable resistance that accompanies disruptions to the status quo, some of it, perhaps, avoidable, and some of it, most certainly, not.

This undertaking has been remarkable in its focus, its comprehensiveness, and its tenacity. Most reform initiatives have been criticized for being partial—attempting to change only one aspect of operations,

such as governance, or curriculum, or evaluation, for example; for rov-
ing from one reform idea to the next in a sort of "flavor of the month"
approach; and for coming and going relatively quickly, with the changing of a superintendent, a board, or a state-policy framework. The San
Diego leadership not only persevered and maintained a holistic approach, it also wrestled with outside influences to use them to the advantage of "inside" purposes without being carried off course by the
force of someone else's momentum.

As this study came to a close, the reform was evolving in a number
of ways, developing a new approach to transforming the structural as
well as pedagogical features of high schools, incorporating lessons
from efforts over the previous several years in new approaches at all
school levels, softening some aspects of standardized policy to accommodate local school contexts and ideas, and deepening practice at the
local school level.

NEGOTIATING DISTRICT AND SCHOOL RELATIONSHIPS

Michael Fullan (1991, p. 200) observes that research has confirmed
that neither centralization nor decentralization works. As he comments
in his summary of research on change:

> Centralization—intensification being the extreme example—does not
> work because it attempts to standardize curriculum and performance in a
> way that is inappropriate and ineffective except for the narrowest goals.
> Decentralization—such as school- or site-based management—is prob-
> lematic either because individual schools lack the capacity to manage
> change or because assessment of attempted changes cannot be tracked.

In San Diego, as in many other districts during the 1980s and early
1990s, advocates of site-based management saw bottom-up decision-
making as a panacea for the ills of bureaucracy. However, by itself, this
strategy led to schools with high capacity becoming stronger and those
with limited capacity often languishing, buffeted by the winds of external forces. Meanwhile, centralizers have often sought to enforce
teacher-proof (and student-proof) curricula—tightly scripted approaches that ignore the need for teacher expertise and preclude local

decision-making. These have generally prevented the classroom adaptations that many students need in order to learn and chased the most capable professionals from the system (Darling-Hammond, 1997b).

Looking for a pathway between this Scylla and Charybdis, Alvarado and Bersin sought to implement the sophisticated notion that a district can use centralized and decentralized strategies to help build professional knowledge and skill that enable principals and teachers to make more nuanced, personalized, and *well-grounded* decisions about how to help individual children. Part of this approach includes proactively organizing resources (dollars, ideas, and people) that can enable schools to improve while shielding them from distractions and impediments. The reform puts on the table questions of *which* decisions should be made at the top, *what* should be standardized and what can be flexible, and *how* various actors should relate to one another in a professional system.

While the road thus far has been rocky, it is clear that in many respects the district's theories of learning, teaching, and the change process are succeeding overall, although to different extents in different parts of the system. At the heart of San Diego's approach is an insistence on seeing the district as a system of schools. Part of the theory of action that Alvarado repeatedly emphasizes is that a system-wide approach is essential to improving quality and equity. As he said at a meeting on the school district's role in building instructional capacity:

> One thing I think I am right about is that if you do something right, you have to do it across the board. Otherwise, the other part of the organization continues, and it eats away at the innovation.

The system-wide approach has, in a short period of time, created new norms and understandings of practice, disrupted patterns of inequity and begun to improve the quality of teaching as well as the level of learning for the students who were previously least well served, and created the beginnings of new capacity and infrastructure for teaching in the district. The district's human capital has improved, and its capacity for offering professional learning has been expanded through the district's reallocation of funds, its development of new vehicles for learning among principals and teachers, and its partnerships with universities and other organizations. Our school-level study suggests that the district has responded to school needs in much the same way it asked schools to respond to students: support those with the greatest needs first. The successes have been most obvious at the elementary level, where the reforms are also most accepted, but they have also made a dent in the middle schools, supporting improvements in previously failing schools, those with uneven practice, and even those with greater strengths. The high school agenda, as we have described, was still evolving. Here, too, however, school principals reported feeling that the revisions in the district's approach—acknowledging the different concerns of high schools and their need for structural as well as pedagogical reforms—were supportive of their needs and of productive change.

Schools' responses to district and state reforms have varied, depending on many aspects of organizational capacity—capacity to marshall professional expertise in the administrative and teaching force, to assist new and veteran teachers in their learning, to foster collaboration, and to offer students a coherent, well-supported school experience. When schools with weak capacity confront competing policy goals and means from different outside forces, they cannot integrate these interventions to support a coherent school approach. Schools with greater capacity are more able to withstand and profitably use outside interventions. For weaker schools, especially, districts are needed to leverage certain resources, including people, time, and expertise, so that the school can respond more productively to policy demands, on the one hand, and develop an internal coherence, on the other.

The district's reforms also extracted some heavy costs, especially in terms of local participation, and in terms of the homogenization of some structures and practices that were previously at least partly successful (e.g., Robinson's houses and close-knit student and teacher teams). As the norms and practices championed by the reform became more institutionalized, there were signs that the district was becoming more comfortable with negotiating flexibility in some aspects of implementation with local schools and more responsive in listening to both concerns and ideas from those in the field, as long as these lay within the parameters of professional practice and equity set out as the goalposts for the work.

Redefining Professionalism

This increased openness may have been occurring in part as a response to strong voices from the field, including the teachers union and educators in the secondary schools, about the need for adaptations. It may have been in part possible because of the "jolt" that created a sense of clarity about purpose and mission and that initiated the process of reculturing. Organizational theory predicts that to the extent there is a stronger set of common norms and values and a deeper level of shared professional knowledge and competence, greater flexibility and professional autonomy can be granted without jeopardizing quality or equity (Benveniste, 1987). As that common knowledge and set of commitments take root, it will follow that more discretion can be granted without concerns that decisions will be made in idiosyncratic ways, uninformed by professional knowledge or a commitment to equitable inputs and outcomes.

Part of the "jolt" concerned a redefinition of professionalism from the notion of *individual autonomy*, even in the absence of professional knowledge or standards of practice, to a notion of *collective responsibility* for knowledge-based practice that attends to questions of principled practice. This notion presumes shared knowledge and authority by members of the profession. While some of the concerns voiced by local practitioners have been associated with the discomfort of making practice public and the insecurity of change, 3 years into the reform we heard very few teachers or principals suggesting that their goal was to revert to a version of individual autonomy that would permit idiosyncratic, frequently ineffective practice. Most were quick to applaud the intent of the reforms and the notions of practice put forward, even if they simultaneously voiced concerns about the speed of change and the processes by which input was or was not sought.

The norms of collective responsibility appeared to be taking hold. This notion was accompanied by the idea of reciprocal accountability for professional practice, voiced by Superintendent Alan Bersin at a principals' conference in 2002:

> Professional review and evaluation is an art and a science and it requires fairness and it requires precision and it requires insight and it requires confidence. And it requires that we learn to use the humanity that is

within us as good leaders not to leave bruises, to be able to make a critical comment in a way that helps the person move forward rather than slide back. The whole essence of what we have attempted to do and will continue to do more strongly is to introduce a notion of reciprocal accountability. You cannot hold someone accountable unless you provide that professional with the skills and knowledge of the tools that they need to have a chance to improve their practice. A person is obligated to improve their practice.

If professionals are obligated to improve their practice, by inference the system is obligated to help them. As the work has taken hold, more and more school-based professionals felt the district's goal was a worthy one and that the direction of the reform is improving their practice. The next steps of the reform would determine whether they also feel they are being heard on what they feel they need and how they feel they can best make that collective journey.

RECALIBRATING REFORM AT THE HIGH SCHOOL LEVEL

As we have noted, high schools present particular challenges to system-wide reform. If the district is the relevant "implementing system" (McLaughlin, 1987, p. 175), then there remains an open question as to how to address the needs of this subset of schools while maintaining district-wide coherence. Reformers in San Diego have managed this within-system variation by keeping high school–specific moves within the parameters of the district's overall reform theory. Even though high schools meet in separate Learning Communities and have more subject areas to attend to, the message remains the same: the goal is to improve student achievement by supporting teaching and learning in the classroom.

The changing tone of the reform at the high school level—one of working with schools rather than doing to them—raised a few important questions. First, was this change in strategy a result of district leaders' learning from experience the importance of engaging principals in reform work, recognition that there is no real model for multiple school instructional improvement at the high school level, or both? Second, by working closely with a subset of high schools—6 of 18—on whole-school reform, was the district creating a divide within the high school ranks that might hamper further efforts at improvement? At each juncture, the district has to balance the issues of system-wide change with local preferences, needs, and initiatives. This process in San Diego, as in every district, is an ongoing dilemma to be managed, not a problem that will be forever solved.

MEDIATING STATE POLICIES

Where state policies threatened to shift the focus of the district or its schools away from locally defined goals, San Diego City Schools committed itself to those goals by subsuming the state policy within the local reform. This strategy is evident in how the district was able to shape the Beginning Teacher Support and Assessment program at the elementary level to reinforce the literacy initiative by using trained literacy coaches as mentors, and in how the district applied portions of the state reading initiative to its own work without compromising its research-based theory of instruction in literacy. With a strong and articulated theory of change against which to evaluate state policies and how they could support or detract from the district's reform agenda, San Diego was able to counter the risk of expending energy in divergent directions to keep up with a state environment of rapid-fire policies.

Instead of being thrown off course by state calls for high school improvement, reformers in San Diego tied many of their local improvement goals to state mandates and university requirements. Indeed, San Diego's leaders appeared to be using these state policies as a warrant to engage schools in the difficult work of high school change. By connecting local goals to those of the state and university system, reformers were able to use exogenous policies as a rationale for improvement and use these external demands as a shield against local resistance to reform. While the accelerated timeline of some state accountability reforms, such as the California High School Exit Exam, might not align with the local agenda, the district nonetheless seemed to be using state reforms in the service of local goals.

Our study suggests that the districts' efforts to forge a coherent reform and mediate state policies had thus far been most successful with respect to the Literacy Framework, had begun to gain traction with respect to mathematics, and had established a toehold in science. The district had also made some headway in leveraging and mediating the state's intrusive accountability policies and beginning-teacher support, although this was more difficult, at least at the secondary level. The handling of each of the three state policies discussed in this book exemplifies one of the tensions we outlined at the start: attending to system-wide needs and school-level differences. San Diego City Schools' theory of change allowed it to ameliorate the state's relatively punitive high-stakes accountability measures to a substantial extent by focusing on investments in schools and students needing greater support, and by prioritizing stronger teachers and teaching for lower-achieving students, rather than by relying largely on sanctions like grade retention that have been found to be counterproductive in many other urban districts. The manner in which the district recast the state accountability policies and intervened to support its neediest schools reaffirmed its commitment to a *tangible* equity in learning opportunities for all students throughout the district. Rather than relying for motivation on the punishment and rewards embodied in the state policies San Diego City Schools offered a more comprehensive view of the knowledge, material, and human resources necessary to enable the lowest-performing schools to better teach their students.

We also found that by holding fast to its own theory of instruction in literacy, the district improved upon the quality of induction and reading as put forth by the state. The state's definition of literacy instruction was much narrower than that of the district. The district's understanding of what it means for students to become engaged readers, the types of learning experiences they must have to become readers, and the pedagogical knowledge teachers must develop to create those learning opportunities was both research based and internally consistent. Importantly, the district's theory of instruction provided a rubric against which to assess the opportunities available from the state (or other providers for that matter) and a unifying force with which to bring coherence to external influences.

POSTSCRIPT: THE ROAD AHEAD

Although our study focused on the early part of San Diego's reform (from 1998 to 2002), there were a number of notable changes in the state and district climate during the 2002–2003 school year that will undoubtedly affect the ultimate outcomes of these initiatives:

- In November 2002, a contentious school board election resulted in a continuation of the 3-2 "pro-reform" majority that had sustained the reform's momentum thus far.
- In December 2002, Chancellor Tony Alvarado announced that he would reduce his role in the district and leave the chancellorship by September 2003.
- In March 2003, SDCS sent layoff notices to 1,487 teachers in response to the state's budget crisis and predicted cuts in class-size reduction monies; in addition, district officials held a series of briefings with certificated, classified, and administrative bargaining groups as well as community members to strategize on imminent budget reductions throughout the winter and spring.
- Also in response to the state budget crisis, the district offered an early retirement package to district employees with an annual benefit bonus of 7% of final-year pay; over 700 teachers and a number of ranking central-office staff accepted, including the directors of counseling and guidance, human resources, and the two instructional leaders assigned to the high schools.
- In June 2003, the school board passed a budget for 2003–2004 that was $65 million less than the prior year's, including $21 million in cuts from the "Blueprint." Over 400 positions were eliminated and over 1,400 employees accepted the retirement plan, allowing the district to rescind all teacher layoff notices.
- Working with the San Diego Education Association, the district passed a 3-year teachers' contract in June 2003, holding salaries and benefits steady for that time period. The negotiations, which were complete before the current contract expired, signaled to some observers an increased spirit of cooperation between the district and the union (*San Diego Union Tribune*, May 2, 2003).
- In the winter of 2002–2003, the two high school Learning Communities were reorganized into "study groups" based on school needs and common reform approaches, such as "community engagement" or "school redesign." A new high school reform administrator was appointed in June 2003.

Clearly, any reforming school district is a "moving target," where improvement efforts will continue to be shaped and reshaped over time.

Yet the sweeping nature of these changes—notably, the departure of Alvarado and the retirement of many district administrators as well as significant belt-tightening across the system—necessarily creates challenges to the institutionalization of the prior years' reforms and raises the question of whether the remaining infrastructure will have the capacity to support the ongoing work.

At a principals' conference at the end of the 2002–2003 school year, both Superintendent Bersin and now-Chief Academic Officer Mary Hopper underscored that the work of raising achievement in the district was far from over and the upcoming year's focus would be on action to improve student outcomes. Only time will tell if the reform's upward trends in K–8 will continue and whether or not the ongoing adjustments to the high school reform approach will result in improved student achievement as measured by district benchmarks. For now, it seems that the district's bet on the power of professional learning to strengthen school practice and performance may rest on whether the district can both sustain and rebuild capacity in the face of significant turnover and budget shortfall. Time will also tell whether the district's intense investment in the knowledge base and skills of the profession has been sufficient to strengthen the ability of local schools to forge their own meaningful learning and teaching agendas that strengthen them from the inside out.

Appendix: San Diego City Schools District-Wide Student Performance, SAT-9

Percentage of Students Scoring at or above the 50th Percentile

Subject	Reading						Mathematics					
Year	1998	1999	2000	2001	2002	% Change 1998–2002	1998	1999	2000	2001	2002	% Change 1998–2002
Students tested	n = 86,635	n = 89,900	n = 88,980	n = 92,644	n = 93,626		n = 89,016	n = 91,383	n = 90,042	n = 93,326	n = 93,789	
Grade												
2	43	50	57	55	61	18	50	56	63	61	64	14
3	41	47	52	49	52	11	46	57	64	61	64	18
4	41	42	48	49	51	10	42	46	56	52	55	13
5	44	44	44	47	49	5	45	47	50	52	55	10
6	43	45	47	48	50	7	47	50	53	52	55	8
7	44	44	48	48	49	5	42	42	46	47	50	8
8	45	48	51	52	52	7	40	43	45	43	46	6
9	36	36	40	38	37	1	48	49	55	53	54	6
10	34	35	37	38	35	1	42	46	52	48	46	4
11	37	38	40	37	40	3	45	49	56	49	51	6
Gr. 2–11	41	44	47	47	48	7	45	49	55	53	54	9

Source: California Department of Education, star.cde.ca.gov/star2002/.

Total Reading: Number and Percent of Students Scoring in Each Quartile on the National Distribution (SAT-9), Grades 2–11 Combined								
	Q1		Q2		Q3		Q4	
Year	#	%	#	%	#	%	#	%
1998	29,867	36	19,739	23	17,654	21	17,090	20
1999	28,280	32	21,058	24	19,047	22	19,106	22
2000	24,901	28	22,242	25	20,292	23	21,511	24
2001	26,737	29	22,661	24	21,541	23	21,677	24
Total	−3,130		+2,922		+3,887		+4,587	

Total Mathematics: Number and Percent of Students Scoring in Each Quartile on the National Distribution (SAT-9), Grades 2–11 Combined								
	Q1		Q2		Q3		Q4	
Year	#	%	#	%	#	%	#	%
1998	26,549	31	21,006	24	18,440	21	20,725	24
1999	23,914	27	21,203	24	19,778	22	24,054	27
2000	19,686	22	21,192	23	20,954	24	28,180	31
2001	22,375	24	21,935	23	21,289	23	27,703	30
Total	−4,174		+929		+2,849		+6,980	

References

Allen, J. & Gonzalez, K. (1998). *There's room for me here: Literacy workshop in the middle school*. York, ME: Stenhouse Publishers.

American Institutes for Research (AIR). (2003). *Evaluation of the blueprint for student success in a standards-based system: Year two interim report*. Palo Alto, CA: Author.

Ball, D., & Cohen, D. (1999). Developing practice, developing practitioners. In L. Darling-Hammond & G. Sykes (Eds.), *Teaching as the learning profession: A handbook of policy and practice*. San Francisco: Jossey-Bass.

Benveniste, G. (1987). *Professionalizing the organization: Reducing bureaucracy to enhance effectiveness*. San Francisco: Jossey-Bass.

Bersin, A. D. (2001, Summer). Reform efforts translate to student and school progress. *The San Diego Union Tribune*. Retrieved August 1, 2001, from http://pqasb.pqarchiver.com/sandiego/mai.

Bodilly, S. J. (1998). *Lessons from New American Schools' scale-up phase: Prospects for bringing designs to multiple schools*. Santa Monica, CA: RAND Corporation.

Bransford, J., Brown, A., & Cocking, R. (1999). *How people learn*. Washington, DC: National Research Council.

California Commission on Teacher Credentialing (CCTC). (2003). *Teacher supply in California: A report to the legislature, fifth annual report, 2001–02*. Sacramento: Author.

California Department of Education (CDE). (2001a). *Statewide enrollment in California public schools by ethnic group, 2000–01*. Retrieved July 11, 2001, from www.data1.cde.ca.gov/dataquest.

California Department of Education (CDE). (2001b). *Number of teachers in California public schools by ethnic designation and gender, 2000–01*. Retrieved July 11, 2001, from www.data1.cde.ca.gov/dataquest.

California Department of Education (CDE). (2001c). *Selected statewide data for the year 2000–01, free or reduced-price meals.* Retrieved February 25, 2002, from www.data1.cde.ca.gov/dataquest.

California Department of Education (CDE). (2001d). *Number of English learners in California public schools, by language and grade ranked by total, 2000–01, statewide.* Retrieved February 25, 2002, from www.data1.cde.ca.gov/dataquest.

California Department of Education (CDE). (2001e). *Classroom teacher credential and experience report by district for the year 2000–01, 3768338—San Diego City Unified.* Retrieved February 25, 2002, from www.data1.cde.ca.gov/dataquest.

California Department of Education (CDE). (2001f). *California reading initiative.* Retrieved February 25, 2002, from www.data1.cde.ca.gov/dataquest.

California Professional Development Task Force. (2001). *Learning, teaching, leading. . . Report of the Professional Development Task Force.* Sacramento: California Department of Education.

Calkins, L. (2001). *The art of teaching reading.* New York: Addison-Wesley.

Carroll, S., Reichardt, R., & Guarino, C. (2000). *The distribution of teachers among California's school districts and schools.* Santa Monica, CA: RAND Corporation.

Center for the Study of Teaching and Policy (CTP). (2000, May 18). *San Diego principal survey results.* Stanford, CA: Author.

Center for the Study of Teaching and Policy (CTP). (2001, Spring). *San Diego Teacher Survey Results.* Stanford, CA: Author.

Christman, J. B., Foley, E., Passantino, C., & Moredecai-Phillips, R. (1998). *Guidance for school improvement in a decentralizing system: How much, what kind, and from where?* Philadelphia: Center for Policy Research in Education.

Cochran-Smith, M., & Lytle, S. L. (1999). Teacher learning in communities. In A. Iran-Nejad & C. D. Pearson (Eds.), *Review of Research in Education, 24.* Washington, DC: American Educational Research Association.

Cohen, D. K., & Hill, H. C. (2000). Instructional policy and classroom performance: The mathematics reform in California. *Teachers College Record, 102*(2), 294–343.

Cuban, L. (1984). *How teachers taught: Constancy and change in American classrooms.* New York: Longman.

Cunningham, A. E., & Stanovich, K. E. (1998, Spring/Summer). What reading does for the mind. *American Educator,* 8–15.

Darling-Hammond, L. (1997a). *Doing what matters most: Investing in quality teaching.* New York: National Commission on Teaching and America's Future.

Darling-Hammond, L. (1997b). *The right to learn.* San Francisco: Jossey-Bass.

Darling-Hammond, L. (1998). Teachers and teaching: Testing policy hypotheses from a National Commission report. *Educational Researcher, 27,* 5–15.

Darling-Hammond, L. (2000a). *Educating teachers for California's future.* San Francisco: The Irvine Foundation.

Darling-Hammond, L. (2000b). Teacher quality and student achievement. *Educational Policy Analysis Archives, 8*(1), http://epaa.asu.edu/epaa/v8n1.

Darling-Hammond, L. (with Alexander, M., & Prince, D.). (2002). *Redesigning schools: What matters and what works.* Stanford, CA: School Redesign Network at Stanford University.

Darling-Hammond, L., Ancess, J., & Ort, S. (2001). Reinventing high school: Outcomes of the coalition campus schools project. *American Educational Research Journal, 39*(3), 639–73.

Darling-Hammond, L., & McLaughlin, M. W. (1999). Investing in teaching as a learning profession: Policy problems and prospects. In L. Darling-Hammond & G. Sykes (Eds.), *Teaching as the learning profession: Handbook of policy and practice* (pp. 376-411). San Francisco: Jossey-Bass.

Darling-Hammond, L., & Sykes, G. (1999). *Teaching as the learning profession: Handbook of policy and practice.* San Francisco: Jossey-Bass.

EdSource. (2001, October). *How California ranks: A comparison of education expenditures.* Palo Alto, CA: EdSource.

Elmore, R. (1983). Complexity and control: What legislators and administrators can do about implementing public policy. In L. Shulman & G. Sykes (Eds.), *Handbook of teaching and policy* (pp. 342–68). New York: Longman.

Elmore, R. F. (1996). Accountability in local school districts: Learning to do the right things. In P. W. Thurston & J. G. Ward, *Improving educational performance: Local and systemic reforms* (Vol. 5, pp. 59–82). Greenwich, CT: JAI Press, Inc.

Elmore, R. F. (2000). *Building a new structure for school leadership.* Washington, DC: Shanker Institute.

Elmore, R. F., & Burney, D. (1999). Investing in teacher learning: Staff development and instructional improvement. In L. Darling-Hammond & G. Sykes (Eds.), *Teaching as the learning profession* (pp. 263–91). San Francisco: Jossey-Bass.

Evans, P. M., & Mohr, N. (1999). Professional development for principals: Seven core beliefs. *Phi Delta Kappa, 80*(7), 530–32.

Fine, M. (Ed.). (1994). *Chartering urban school reform: Reflections on public high schools in the midst of change.* New York: Teachers College Press.

Firestone, W. A. (1989). Using reform: Conceptualizing district initiative. *Educational Evaluation and Policy Analysis, 11*(2), 151–64.

Fountas, I. C., & Pinnell, G. S. (1996). *Guided reading: Good first teaching for all children.* Portsmouth, NH: Heinemann Press.

Fullan, M. G. (1991). *The new meaning of educational change.* New York: Teachers College Press.

Fullan, M. G. (1993). *Change forces: Probing the depths of educational reform.* Bristol, PA: The Falmer Press.

Guthrie, J. W., & Sanders, T. (2001, January 7). Who will lead the public schools? *The New York Times*, p. N46.

Hightower, A. M. (2001). *San Diego's big boom: District bureaucracy meets culture of learning.* Unpublished doctoral dissertation, Stanford University, California.

Hightower, A. M. (2002a). *San Diego's big boom: District bureaucracy supports culture of learning.* (Center for the Study of Teaching and Policy Report No. R-02-2). Seattle: University of Washington Press.

Hightower, A. M. (2002b). San Diego's big boom: Systemic instructional change in the central office and schools. In A. Hightower, M. Knapp, J. Marsh, & M. McLaughlin (Eds.), *School districts and instructional renewal.* New York: Teachers College Press.

Hightower, A. M., Marsh, J. A., Talbert, J. T., & Wechsler, M. E. (2000). *The district role in school improvement: Bringing bottom-up perspectives into the dialogue.* Presentation at the annual meeting of the American Educational Research Association, New Orleans.

Hightower, A. M., & McLaughlin, M. W. (2002). Traveling ideas: Knowledge-management in San Diego City Schools. Paper presented at the annual meeting of the American Educational Research Association, New Orleans.

Hill, P., Campbell, C., & Harvey, J. (2000). *It takes a city: Getting serious about urban school reform.* Washington, DC: Brookings Institution Press.

Kain, T. J., & Staiger, D. O. (2001). Volatility in school test scores: Implications for test-based accountability systems. *Accountability and its consequences for students: Are children helped or hurt by standards-based reforms?* Symposium presented at the Brookings Institution, Washington, DC.

Koppich, J. E., & Knapp, M. S. (1998). *Federal research investment and the improvement of teaching 1980–1997.* Seattle: University of Washington Press.

Lindblom, C. E. (1980). *The policy-making process* (2nd ed.). Englewood Cliffs, NJ: Prentice-Hall.

Linn, R. L., & Haug, C. (2002). Stability of school-building accountability scores and gains. *Educational Evaluation and Policy Analysis, 24*(1): 29–36.

Little Hoover Commission. (2001, September). *Teach our children well.* Retrieved from http://www.lhc.ca.gov/lhcdire/160report160.pdf.

Little, J. W. (1990). The persistence of privacy: Autonomy and initiative in teachers' professional relations. *Teachers College Record, 91*(4), 509–36. New York: Teachers College Press.

Little, J. W. (1993). Teachers' professional development in a climate of educational reform. *Educational Evaluation and Policy Analysis, 15*(2), 129–51.

Little, J. W. (1999). Organizing schools for teacher learning. In L. Darling-Hammond & G. Sykes (Eds.), *Teaching as the learning profession: Handbook of policy and practice* (pp. 376–411). San Francisco: Jossey-Bass.

Lortie, D. (1975). *Schoolteacher: A sociological study.* Chicago: University of Chicago Press.

March, J. G., & Simon, H. A. (1958). *Organizations.* New York: John Wiley.

McLaughlin, M. W. (1987). Learning from experience: Lessons from policy implementation. *Educational Evaluation and Policy Analysis, 9*(2), 171–178.

McLaughlin, M. W., & Oberman, I. (Eds.). (1996). *Teacher learning: New policies, new practices.* New York: Teachers College Press.

McLaughlin, M. W., & Talbert, J. (2001). *Professional communities and the work of high school teaching.* Chicago: University of Chicago Press.

McLaughlin, M. W., Talbert, J. E., Crowe, B. Roller, C., Ebby, R., Ikeda, K., Mitra, D., Moffett, K., & Zarrow, J. (1999). *Asessing results: The Bay Area School Reform Collaborative.* Standford, CA: Center for Research on the Context of Teaching.

Mehan, H., & Grimes, S. (1999). *Measuring the achievement gap in San Diego City Schools.* San Diego: University of California, San Diego.

Meyer, J. W., Scott, W. R., & Strang, D. (1994). Centralization, fragmentation, and school district complexity. In W. R. Scott, J. W. Meyer, & Associates (Eds.), *Institutional environments and organizations* (pp. 160–78). Thousand Oaks, CA: Sage.

Miles, K. H., & Darling-Hammond, L. (1998). Rethinking the allocation of teaching resources: Some lessons from high-performing schools. *Educational Evaluation and Policy Analysis, 20*(1), 9–29.

Miles, K. H., & Guiney, E. (2000, June 14). School districts' new role. *Education Week 19*(40): 30, 32–33.

National Center for Education Statistics (NCES). (1999). *Teacher quality: A report on the preparation and qualifications of public school teachers.* Washington, DC: U.S. Department of Education.

National Council of Teachers of Mathematics (NCTM). (1989). *Curriculum and evaluation standards for school mathematics.* Reston, VA: Author.

Oakes, J. (1985). *Keeping track: How schools structure inequality.* New Haven: Yale University Press.

O'Day, J. A., & Smith, M. S. (1993). Systemic school reform and educational opportunity. In S. Fuhrman (Ed.), *Designing coherent educational policy: Improving the system* (pp. 250–312). San Francisco: Jossey-Bass.

Powell, A. G., Farrar, E., & Cohen, D. K. (1985). *The shopping mall high school: Winners and losers in the educational marketplace.* Boston: Houghton Mifflin.

Putnam, R. T., & Borko, H. (2000). What do new views of knowledge and thinking have to say about research on teacher learning? *Educational Researcher, 29*(1), 4–15.

Quick, H., Birman, B., Gallagher, L., Wolman, J., Chaney, K., & Hikawa, H. (2003, July 31). *Evaluation of the blueprint for student success in a standards-based system. Year two interim report.* Palo Alto, CA: American Institutes for Research.

Raywid, M. A., & Schmerler, G. (2003). *Not so easy going: The policy environments of small urban schools and schools-within-schools.* Charleston, WV: ERIC Clearinghouse on Rural Education and Small Schools.

Reichardt, R. (2000). Teacher characteristics. In B. M. Stecher & G. W. Bohrnstedt (Eds.), *Class size reduction in California: The 1998–99 evaluation findings.* Sacramento: California Department of Education.

Resnick, L. B. (1995). From aptitude to effort: A new foundation for our schools. *Daedalus, 124*, 55–62.

Resnick, L. B., & Hall, M. W. (1998). Learning organizations for sustainable education reform. *Daedalus, 127*, 89–118.

Rosenholtz, S. J. (1991). *Teachers' workplace: The social organization of schools.* New York: Teachers College Press.

San Diego Achievement Forum. (2002, October). *Achievement in San Diego City Schools: A progress report.* San Diego: Author.

San Diego City Schools (SDCS). (2000, April 20). *Schools for a New Society proposal application.* San Diego: Author.

San Diego City Schools (SDCS). (2001, August 1). *San Diego high schools achieving rigorous performance: A proposal to the Carnegie Corporation's Schools for a New Society initiative.* San Diego: Author.

San Diego City Schools (SDCS). (2002a, February). *San Diego Smaller Learning Communities Initiative: Implementation grant proposal.* San Diego: Author.

San Diego City Schools (SDCS). (2002b, March). *Status report on district high school reform efforts.* San Diego: Author.

San Diego City Schools (SDCS). (2003a, Fall). *Fact Sheet: Mathematics Framework.* San Diego: Author.

San Diego City Schools (SDCS). (2003b, September). *Status report on district high school reform.* San Diego: Author.

San Diego School Board. *Blueprint for student success.* San Diego: San Diego Board of Education.

Sebring, P. B., Bryk, A.S., & Easton, J. Q. (1995). *Charting reform: Chicago teachers take stock.* Chicago: Consortium on Chicago School Research.

Shields, P. M., Esch, C. E., Humphrey, D. C., Young, V. M., Gaston, M., & Hunt, H. (1999). The status of the teaching profession: Research findings and recommendations. A report to the Teaching and California's Future Task Force. Santa Cruz, CA: Center for the Future of Teaching and Learning.

Shields, P. M., Humphrey, D. C., Wechsler, M. E., Riehl, L. M., Tiffany-Morales, J., Woodworth, K., Young, V. M., & Price, T. (2001). *Teaching and California's future: The status of the teaching profession 2001.* Santa Cruz, CA: The Center for the Future of Teaching and Learning.

Siskin, L. S., & Lemons, R. (2000). *Internal and external accountability: The challenge of the high school.* Paper presented at the Annual Meeting of the American Educational Research Association, New Orleans.

Siskin, L. S., & Little, J. W. (Eds.). (1995). *The subjects in question: Departmental organization and the high school.* New York: Teachers College Press.

Sonstelie, J., Brunner, E., & Ardon, K. (2000). *1946—For better or for worse?: School finance reform in California.* San Francisco: Public Policy Institute of California.

Spillane, J. P., Halverson, R., & Diamond, J. B. (2001). Investigating school leadership practice: A distributed perspective. *Educational Researcher, 30*(3), 23–28.

Stein, M. K., & D'Amico, L. (2000, April). *How subjects matter in school leadership.* Paper presented at the annual meeting of the American Educational Research Association, New Orleans.

Stein, M. K., & D'Amico, L. (2002). The district as professional learning laboratory. In A. M. Hightower, M. S. Knapp, J. A. Marsh, & M. W. McLaughlin (Eds.), *School districts and instructional renewal: Opening the conversation* (pp. 61–75). New York: Teachers College Press.

Stein, M. K., Smith, M. S., & Silver, E. A. (1999). The development of professional developers: Learning to assist teachers in new settings in new ways. *Harvard Educational Review, 69*(3), 237–69.

Sykes, G. (1999). Introduction: Teaching as the learning profession. In L. Darling-Hammond & G. Sykes (Eds.), *Teaching as the learning profession.* San Francisco: Jossey-Bass.

Tushman, M. L., & O'Reilly, C. A. (1996, Summer). Ambidextrous organizations: Managing evolutionary and revolutionary change. *California Management Review, 38*(4), 8–30.

Wilson, S., Darling-Hammond, L., & Berry, B. (2001). *Connecticut: A case of successful teaching policy.* University of Washington: Center for the Study of Teaching and Policy.

Wilson, S. M., & Berne, J. (1999). Teacher learning and the acquisition of professional knowledge: An examination of research on contemporary professional development. *Review of Research in Education, 24*, 173–209.

Index

About the Authors

Linda Darling-Hammond is Charles E. Ducommun Professor of Education at Stanford University where she is also faculty sponsor for the Stanford Teacher Education Program and codirector of the Stanford Education Leadership Institute. Her research, teaching, and policy interests focus on educational policy, school redesign, teacher quality, and educational equity. She is author or editor of 10 other books, including *The Right to Learn: A Blueprint for Creating Schools that Work*, and more than 200 journal articles, book chapters, and monographs on issues of educational policy and practice.

Amy M. Hightower studied the district reform initiative underway in San Diego City Schools from 1998–2001 while pursuing her doctorate at Stanford University. She is currently an assistant director at the American Federation of Teachers working on labor/management collaborations and accountability.

Jennifer L. Husbands is a research assistant at the Center for Research on the Context of Teaching at Stanford University and has conducted research in San Diego as a member of the Center for the Study of Teaching and Policy. Her work focuses on the reform of comprehensive high schools, with particular emphasis on the role of school and district leadership in high school reform in urban settings.

Jeannette R. LaFors is a Ph.D. candidate in education policy at Stanford University and a research assistant at the Center for the Study of

Teaching and Policy. She formerly taught social studies in the Sequoia Union High School District in California. Her research focuses on school-level instructional leadership, with a particular emphasis on the relationship between school principals' conceptions of teacher quality and their actions as instructional leaders.

Viki M. Young is a Ph.D. candidate in education policy at Stanford University and a research assistant at the Center for Research on the Contexts of Teaching. She formerly served as an education policy analyst at SRI International. Her research centers on teachers' use of data for instructional purposes, and the organizational and policy conditions that shape teachers' practices.

Carl Christopher is associate director for finance and outreach of the Center for Teacher Education and School Reform at Stanford University. He graduated from University of California at San Diego in 1998 with a degree in economics and began his career in economic development, working on the promotion of relationships between the business and education sectors.